The Boy From Back Creek,

The Girl From 531 Pelham Street

Also by James E. Casey, Jr.

From Rags To Riches

The Shepherd and His Sheep

The Boy From Back Creek,
The Girl From 531 Pelham Street

*The True Story of Two People
Seeking to Please the Heavenly Father*

by

James E. Casey, Jr.

Edited by
May G. Onishchuk

The Boy From Back Creek, The Girl From 531 Pelham Street
© 2012 by James E. Casey, Jr.

All rights reserved. No part of this book may be reproduced in any form or by any electronic or mechanical means including information storage and retrieval systems, without permission in writing from the author. The only exception is by a reviewer, who may quote short excerpts in a review.

Edited by May G. Onishchuk and J. Lyndon Casey
Cover and Interior design by J. Lyndon Casey

Unless otherwise indicated, all Scriptures noted are taken from the KING JAMES VERSION of the HOLY BIBLE.

Scriptures noted NKJV are taken from the NEW KING JAMES VERSION®. © 1982 by Thomas Nelson, Inc. Used by permission. All rights reserved. NKJV is a trademark of Thomas Nelson, Inc.

Scriptures noted NIV are taken from THE HOLY BIBLE, NEW INTERNATIONAL VERSION®, © 1973, 1978, 1984, 2011 by Biblical, Inc.™ Used by permission. All rights reserved worldwide.

Printed in the United States of America
ISBN 978-0-615-70602-3

Dedication

This is book is dedicated to the memory of my wife Oleta Lancaster Casey. She stood by me day and night no matter where I was.

"Who can find a virtuous woman? for her price is far above rubies. The heart of her husband doth safely trust in her, so that he shall have no need of spoil. She will do him good and not evil all the days of her life" (Proverbs 31:10–12).

Contents

As I See It xi

Foreword xiii

Preface xv

Acknowledgement xvii

Introduction xxi

Early Beginning 1

An Environment For Success 11

College Doors Open 15

Secrets To Success 21

The Mission Field Beckons 25

Giant Steps In Mission Work 29

New Ministry In The Mountains 35

Mission In A Coal Mining Town 41

Comfortable Only For A While 47

A Girl Keeps Reappearing 51

Responding to God 57

Time For Life's Partner 61

A New Starting Point 65

The Wedding 69

The Phelps Mission Is Born 77

A Rock In The Mountains 85

The Home Front 95

A Time To Move On...................................101

The Call To Wheelwright 109

On To West Liberty 117

Reaching Across The State Line 125

A New Challenge..147

Return To Kentucky 163

Director Of Missions 179

Mission Trips Abroad.................................201

Director Of Missions Continued.................209

Retirement—Yet Lots To Do 217

My Aging Mother And Father 233

Closing Years 237

In The Middle Of A Storm 243

The Call To Obey 247

The Horrors Of Hell 253

She's Worth More Than Jewels 261

Epilogue 269

Co-Laborers Give Their Perspectives 271

Correspondence One 271

Correspondence Two 272

Correspondence Three 273

Correspondence Four 274

Correspondence Five...275

Correspondence Six 276

Correspondence Seven...277

Correspondence Eight 277

Correspondence Nine 278

Correspondence Ten..278

Correspondence Eleven 279

Correspondence Twelve...279

Correspondence Thirteen...281

Correspondence Fourteen 282

Correspondence Fifteen 283

Correspondence Sixteen 283

Correspondence Seventeen 284

As I See It

You will be amazed at the kind of good things that will happen to a person when he begins living with faith in Almighty God. You will be reading what is simply a help to encourage people to enjoy the true blessings that come from following the teachings of God's Word. In a short time you will see how to use the power and authority of God's Word.

This book is a reliable and credible history of a family that sold out to rely on faith. It is with much satisfaction that I present to you this vivid narrative of the life and times of my parents and my family.

J. Lyndon Casey
Assistant Editor

Foreword

My grandfather has written this book to show his dedicated life with Jesus Christ. As you read this let Jesus fill your soul.

In this book, my grandfather will tell you about his ancestors, his life as a boy, and where he lived. You will learn about his college days and how it changed his life forever. You will see how he met my grandmother, fell in love, and got married. Then you will learn about their life together with Jesus.

This is a wonderful story about my grandparents, their life together, their adventures, and most of all their faith in God. My grandfather has a lot to share with you, so please get in a nice, comfy place to read and enjoy The Boy From Back Creek, The Girl From 531 Pelham Street.

Christine A. Casey

Preface

I first heard of Jim and Oleta Casey during the final months of 2003, when my husband and I were called to serve at Grand Island Baptist Church. While interviewing and courting this church for a period of 6 months or so, we were told about a wonderful couple who had retired from ministry, but were far from the standard definition of retirement! Their ministry continued within their home, their church and their community. It was only a couple of hours after we were officially voted into the church in early 2004 that we had Jim and Oleta praying over us and sharing with us about the ministry opportunities that were then at our feet.

Jim and Oleta never tried to push their opinions on us but were always willing to share insight on ministerial situations. I remember our first Valentine Make It Take It held at Grand Island. Oleta graciously volunteered to help me with the children. We had three children in attendance: one was her granddaughter and the other two were my boys. She told me, "Don't be discouraged, the Lord will provide!" She shared a wonderful devotional of God's love that which fell upon the hearts of those three children. Those three have been missionaries in our little community and have helped to grow our ministry at Grand Island. Our 2012 Valentine Make It Take It grew from those first three, to over fifty in attendance. I know Jim has helped my husband get his bearings on the nursing homes in this area and was always quick to hand out gospel tracts as he passed people in the hallways of the health care facilities.

Jim and Oleta have always looked for opportunities to minister. This book of their life stories as partners in ministry will be a blessing to all who come across it. The Casey's have always been a good example to my husband and me and now that example can be shared with many more who read about their life and ministry among these pages.

JulieAnn Feezor

Acknowledgement

The Holy Bible has been my guide in this great undertaking. At times it has been an agonizing experience. However, I count it all joy!

I am grateful to all who jumped into the midst of the battle and provided strength and encouragement.

A great number of friends urged me to undertake this task. Not only was it important they said for historical records, but they felt there were lessons for others to be learned from the ministry Almighty God had entrusted into the hands of Oleta and me.

Oleta Lancaster Casey was my beloved wife and companion for over a half a century. Oleta, next to God's grace, was the best thing that ever happened to me.

Our children, Sibyl, Lyndon, Jeffrey, and Barry, and our six grandchildren, Erica, Zachary, Shelby, Rachel, Gillian, and Christine, are all gifts from God and stood tall for Almighty God in this project.

I am truly grateful for Don Stricklin, my son–in–law, who helped to transcribe my hand–written notes for May Onishchuk and Lyndon Casey. He went far and beyond the call–of–duty to make sure that May and Lyndon received all my notes by email. His advice and attention to details were unmatched.

I am deeply indebted to May G. Onishchuk, the editor–in–chief of this book, who was an inspiration to Oleta and me while we lived in Florida and who was so willing to bring together all of this material with remarkable style. May spent many hours diligently organizing and revising this book for the world to read. Her unfailing love and devotion to Almighty God and Kingdom Ministry is beyond all measure.

I would like to acknowledge my son, Lyndon Casey, the assistant editor, for his extraordinary computer skills. He carefully coordinated the materials and skillfully managed the publication of this book. He collaborated with May Onishchuk and worked tirelessly to see this was a finished project.

My daughter, Sibyl Stricklin, had done much to get this book published and for that I am eternally thankful. She insisted Dr. Betty Herron proofread this book to make corrections and suggestions about the content of this book. Dr. Betty Herron holds several degrees from outstanding universities across America and is now retired Professor of Education at the University of the Cumberlands in Williamsburg, Kentucky. I am very thankful for Dr. Betty Herron and her skillful touch to this book.

My pals and fellow travelers along the way who have contributed so much to the book and the work of our Lord.

A special recognition is due to Mr. Henry F. Haas of Mount Dora, Florida. He is a long time friend of Oleta and me. Henry is a prayer warrior and stood in the trenches for the Casey family. On several occasions Mr. Haas drove to Kentucky to be at the side of Oleta and me, and to minister in the time of crisis.

Now to those that will read this book, I have prayed for you, long before you held it in your hands.

I am honored to have all that will read these pages.

May Almighty God hold you firmly in His hands.

Introduction

This book has been written in response to so many suggestions by friends to my wife and me who have heard us relate incidents of answered prayers during our fifty-four years, five months, and two days of married life and ministry in God's work.

I never thought as a little boy growing up in the Depression of the 1930's, on Back Creek in Shelby County, Kentucky, I would ever write a book.

For one thing, I knew it would be beyond my ability to write such a work alone. I have not depended upon my memory alone, but all I have written is fresh on my mind. I have notes which were made at the time and letters which describe many of the experiences.

I realize that it is important that this historical record be made public and used to glorify Almighty God. My prayer is that all who have assisted me will in some way be blessed by the Father in Heaven because of their contributions to this cause.

I really believe God has given me the right people to now assist in this task. This volume is really a labor of love and it is being sent on this journey with the prayer that lives of those who read it may be enriched and blessed by God.

As I look back over the sixty-one years since I was licensed to the Gospel Ministry by the Mount Moriah Baptist

Church of Mount Eden, Kentucky, on June 10, 1951, I must give all the glory and praise to Almighty God.

In these pages I am trying to be as accurate as possible in recalling all of the wonderful days with Oleta and my family.

The preparation for this book has not been an easy task and I am so thankful for all the prayers and moral support given to me by my friends and family.

I will be simply talking to you in my own style—like a fireside talk. You will like it as I tell it just as it was.

Jim Casey

Chapter 1
Early Beginning

As a child develops, we ponder and wonder, what makes that little one who he is becoming? Which habits are ingrained by family genes, which by where and when he is born, which simply by rote? As I matured, God seemed at hand on every turn, nurturing me through the power of the Holy Spirit. I, Jim Casey, learned about God early and soon became very learned in His Word, the Bible—and believed it! I read that God helps His children if they trust in Him, and I saw that equation lived out. Doing that, this is what happened.

To know me is to perhaps know something of my beginnings. My great-grandfather, Reuben Turner Casey, who was born November 14, 1846, lived in Anderson County, Kentucky. It was after the Civil War, about 1866, that he married Alice Jane Gilpin, who was born March 8, 1848. They dreamed of a better day for themselves and their family. They longed to serve the Lord in peace and rear a good and godly family. They settled near a small town called Sinai which is located in Anderson County. Although it was a rough and rugged area to farm, the rolling hills of Kentucky offered many kinds of opportunities for a working man. Sinai seemed like a good place to raise a family as well.

Times were hard for Reuben and Alice but they were hard working, God-fearing people, and to them nothing seemed impossible. The Lord blessed them with a wonderful family.

Their first son, George William was born in the year of 1867. A second son, Gustavus T. 'Gus', was born May 5, 1869. A third son, James Henry, was born June 11, 1872 and on July 15, 1873, Porter, was born. Joseph Robert 'Joe Bob', the fifth son, was born June 15, 1875. Francis Marion 'Frank' was born October 2, 1877, their sixth son. Their seventh son, William 'Will', was born around March of 1881. The only girl, Ora, was born July 29, 1882. Then on April 16, 1886 their eighth son, Charles Tyler, was born. It seems that every member of Reuben's family desired to be somebody. As soon as the children were old enough to be on their own, they struck out to find their own gold mine and from sunrise until dark they worked, prayed, and worked. (See John 15:7 and Romans 8:26). With a few pots, pans, cooking utensils and the best farming tools of that day, James Henry, Frank, and Joe Bob headed for the Bluegrass of Shelby County, Kentucky. Early in life, their parents had instilled in them faith in Almighty God and they never turned back. Like Abraham of the Bible, they ventured out beyond their Sinai habitat in Anderson County to see what opportunities availed them. Both my great-grandparents were Baptists and in 1916 gave property to construct the Friendship Baptist Church on U.S. Highway 62 near Lawrenceburg, Kentucky.

My grandfather was James Henry Casey. He was born on the Sinai homestead and as soon as he was old enough to hold a gun in his hand he was his own man. James Henry was hard working and wanted to be a part of the growing Kentucky. Logging was much a part of the developing area so he pursued

Chapter 1   Early Beginning

it as part of his business. In this same area of Shelby County, where the Casey boys were settling to work and produce a better way of life, they came in contact with the Carpenter family. Little did they know that from this family two of the Casey boys would find future wives.

Reuben Dudley Carpenter was born November 11, 1849 in Shelby County. He fell in love with Judith Frances Watts who was born August 8, 1852, in Shelby County. They were married on October 1, 1871. God blessed them with the following children: James William, born October 15, 1873; Lydia Frances, born February 8, 1881; Anna Mae 'Annie', born October 3, 1883; Sarah Elizabeth 'Bettie', born March 13, 1886; George Ezra, born April 12, 1888; Addie Cleo, born March 28, 1890. Reuben and Judith had three other children who died early in life.

The Carpenter family was one of the most devoted Christian families in the community. From this family many well–educated people have come to bless America, such as teachers, ministers, statesmen, journalists, and international missionaries. (See 1 John 3:22).

It was here in Shelby County that my grandfather, James Henry, met fifteen–year–old Lydia Frances Carpenter on Back Creek, a farming locale near a small rural town called Mount Eden. On January 6, 1897, James Henry and Lydia were married in Shelby County, but they spent their first few years of married life near the Salt River in Spencer County. It was here that their first child, Ernest Clifford, was born on October

4, 1897. God was good to James Henry and Lydia. In 1893 they returned to Shelby County and purchased a small tract of land with a small three-room house. It was just a few hundred yards from a swiftly flowing Little Beech Creek and laid just across from the Carpenter property. It seemed that the blessings from their faith in God was falling upon them. He was prospering in his farming. Not far from the house on joining property was a small cool spring that would furnish them with a good supply of water. In a short while he built a small cellar, a rock wall behind the house, and dug a well near the kitchen for his wife. He soon enlarged the dwelling house so it would be a heavenly place for his wife and family. On September 17, 1899, the Lord blessed them with another son, Meredith Reuben, who everyone called Pete. (See Hebrews 11:6 and James 1:5–7).

James Henry's brother, Frank, fell in love with Annie Carpenter and they were married on January 24, 1900. They settled down on a piece of land he had purchased not far from the Carpenter family. It would be here that he would start his family and faithfully serve the Lord. After many years of hard work and wise planning, Frank and Annie would move near Shelbyville, Kentucky, where they would spend the rest of their days. It seemed God was moving fast in James and Lydia's life for some reason and on April 4, 1902, God placed in their hands a little baby girl. They named her Velma Francis. This beautiful little flower's life was snuffed out by diphtheria a little over a year later in October 1903. They laid her to rest in the Mt. Moriah Cemetery in Mt Eden. The great God of the

Chapter 1 — Early Beginning

universe, who James Henry and Lydia loved and served, smiled upon them and gave them another daughter, Ethel Jane, on November 14, 1904.

James Henry was strong and willing to work hard, and he was soon able to purchase additional land from the Johnson family, who were adjoining neighbors. Now he would have room to raise larger crops, expand his farming, and provide for his family in the future.

He was busy every day of his life either from farming or running the sawmill and gristmill, a place where grain is ground into flour. The mills were located just a few miles up the road from his house at a village called Junte on a narrow stretch of land between Mount Eden and Harrisonville. The mills served the needs of many people in the surrounding communities. In a way, it looked like the Lord blessed everything that James Henry put his hand on. He was happy, his wife was satisfied, and his family was growing. (See Psalm 37:23).

James Henry and Lydia were blessed with another son, James Elmo, on August 27, 1907. As James Henry looked upon this good family God had given him, he knew he would have to struggle hard to provide for their daily needs.

It looked as though God was moving him to new places and to bigger things in the timber industry and there was always the constant call for him to fire-up the sawmill or gristmill to help his neighbors in the community. He had a heart to help people and he never turned anyone away who had a need. For the first time in his life he felt the hand of God on his tired legs and back. This kind of drive to help people in need made him feel good inside. He and his wife could lie down at night knowing that the God of Psalm 23 was with them every day of their life.

Their family was not yet complete. On February 20, 1910, Lydia had another son called Everett Milton. James Henry and Lydia now had four boys and one girl to care for and raise. He knew he would have to work overtime to see that they had the best he could provide.

On the morning of February 8, 1913, James Henry received a call from one of his neighbors who said he needed some corn ground. He was tired from the hard work on the farm, but he could not reject the call to help someone. It was also wintertime and that was when the motors in the mill were often difficult to start. Fighting the cold weather is a tough job. James Henry was a good business man and a good neighbor so he took on the job. He asked his two older sons, Ernest and Pete, to go along so they could assist him. They arrived at the mill site, which was some two miles from their house. After preparing the mill they were able to begin grinding the corn.

James Henry and his boys were anxious to get back home because of the blasting cold. My grandfather quite often stopped the mill motor by pushing the belt off with his foot. It was quicker than going around to the other side and pulling the lever to stop the motor. Today, however, his foot missed the belt and his body was thrown into the belt loop and he was killed instantly. He died before his boys' eyes.

Chapter 1 Early Beginning

The funeral director had his body carried back to the house to be received by a grieving young wife and a crying family. James Henry was laid to rest with his daughter in the Mt. Moriah Cemetery. No person is ever able to answer why such a terrible thing like this happens, but life must go on. That is exactly what happened in the Casey family. Lydia took up the mantel and never looked back. Her devotion to her family, her church, and to her Lord was evident in every aspect of her life. Each member of the family, regardless of their age, had to deal with it. Still, there were days of loneliness and discouragement in the family because the head of the house was gone forever.

My father, James Elmo, was the third son in the family. He often told me that there were no more presents at birthdays or Christmas since the death of his father. It was hard times for every one. Their mother loved them, but there was no income to buy anything extra. There were five mouths to feed three times a day and she was trying to put clothes on their backs as well as send them to school. My father tells of walking up creeks and hollows for about two miles to a one–room school on Back Creek. There were no official roads, just paths where folks rode a horse or traveled by wagon or buggy. One had to be skillful pushing away weeds and briars, and crossing creeks. This is where my father learned the three R's—reading, writing, and arithmetic. He recalled he stopped at a store in Junte and bought a slate to write on for a dime. Eventually, he found his way to the much larger school at Mount Eden.

Schools in the area often had pie sales and ice cream suppers which helped support school activities. In 1925, it was at one of these ice cream suppers at Harrisonville, about eight miles from where my father lived, that he met the girl he would later marry. My father was so attracted to this pretty young girl that he got her name, age, and address in short time. Her name was Edna Mae Frazier who was born on March 24, 1908, and lived with her parents—Everett and Maud Frazier—at the head waters of Back Creek. Elmo, as he was called, had a good horse and buggy, so it wasn't long until he received permission from Edna's parents to court their daughter. Neither family was financially strong but both had a deep faith in God.

Edna was a believer in Almighty God and had committed her life to Him in a revival at Pigeon Fork Baptist Church where Clarence Walker and his brother Walter were preaching. Elmo attended the Mount Moriah Baptist Church in Mount Eden where his mother was a member. She was committed to God and faithfully took her family to church.

Their courtship was swift and short, because Elmo and Edna were ready to launch out on their own. They traveled to Shelbyville and purchased a marriage license. On January 20, 1927, they stood before Dr. C. W. Elsey, pastor of the First Baptist Church of Shelbyville, and were united in Holy Marriage. After the ceremony was over, the groom revealed he had only four dollars in his pocket. The first year of my parents' marriage was spent with Edna's parents. My dad and

Chapter 1 — Early Beginning

Mr. Frazier were partners in cropping that year and they did not break even.

Even though times seemed to be hard for this young couple, they decided to move out on their own. Elmo found a three-room dwelling with dirt floors, which belonged to James Bruner. They moved in and soon afterwards their first child, Virginia Louise, was born on October 27, 1927.

In the winter of 1928, not long after they settled in Back Creek, Edna took sick with a very bad case of pneumonia. Country folk used their own remedies. Some of them worked and some did not. As a young boy, I can remember going out and cutting sassafras bark and roots to make tea for certain ailments. After all the family and neighbors could do to make my mother well, my father called a doctor who lived in Waddy, which was about twenty miles away. Doctors traveled by horse back in those days. The good doctor finally arrived and stayed quite some time trying to do all he could to save her life. Hours passed and finally the good doctor looked up and with tears streaming down his face said, "Elmo, she ain't going to last very long." Then he shook my dad's hand and left, riding away on his big horse.

It was a dark time for my dad and the future was very cloudy. He had not changed clothes in days and had hardly been out of the room for he remembered he had stood before a man of God and promised that he would be with his wife until death. As he turned to the wall in the small bedroom, he whispered a prayer and it seemed that God assured him everything would be alright. (See John 14:13–14).

The next morning at daybreak, my mother opened her eyes for the first time in days. It was indeed as if everything would be alright. It would be several months before my mother would recover her health and spirit. A miracle did happen! My dad was so excited and thankful that he was ready to make another move. God had given him a vision of what could be done in the future and he was ready to go. When I think of how it must have been eating at his heart, I think of the words from the old hymn "Ready". Listen to the words—

> Ready to go, ready to stay,
> Ready my place to fill;
> Ready for service, lowly or great,
> Ready to do His will.

Chapter 2

An Environment For Success

One day when spring was approaching in 1929, Elmo expressed his plan of their future to Edna as he hitched up his horse to the buggy. He wanted to go down to see if he could make a deal with Mam, as he always called his mother, about running the farm for her. He first asked Edna if that was a suitable idea for her. She said she was ready to go with him. Mam agreed to have her son and his family share in half of the house, and to have her son run the farm in a business–like way. It was a good deal for her and it was an opportunity for Elmo to exercise his talents in farm development. He assumed full responsibility for the farm and set out to make it a model in the community. He built fences and barns, and he cleared the land for crops every year.

Edna had prayed for a son, much like Hannah did in the Old Testament, and the Lord did give her and Elmo a little baby boy. It was in this setting, the same house in which my father was born, that I was born on September 4, 1930. They named me James Elmo, after my father, but everyone called me June, which was short for Junior. My mother was so thrilled and excited that she wanted to get me involved in church as soon as possible. My mother taught me Bible stories and grounded me in the word of our Lord. My parents were members of the Mount Moriah Baptist Church, which was only a couple of miles away in Mount Eden. I was just over a year old when my mother enrolled me in the Cradle Department of the Mount Moriah Baptist in Mount Eden on September 29, 1931.

It was the beginning of what is now called the Great Depression. It had just hit Shelby County and it brought hardship to the Casey family. The Bank of Mount Eden had to close and it never opened again. What the farmers had to sell from the farm was of little value. The quietness of the country life taught me to depend on the Lord for everything in life. We were poor, but God was real to us every day.

By 1936, my father felt a good harvest of corn and wheat could basically keep the family fed. My mother would raise a garden and preserve food for the winter. We could raise chickens and sell the eggs at ten cents a dozen. That profit could buy school supplies. If my father could sell a calf, we might be able to use the money for school clothes. My parents firmly believed education was essential and I would be six and ready for school. Everyone had to pitch in and use every resource. Also, the summer of 1936 was dry and hot. Crops were poor. We had to tighten our belts even more. We lost the use of our car as my father could not afford the license tag. But as school bells rang that September, I was enrolled in first grade.

As a twelve year old boy, I remember digging post holds in which to set posts for ten cents a hole and those holes had to be two feet deep. I set traps to catch weasels, opossums, skunks, minks, rabbits or even a fox. I would get up and go to my traps

Chapter 2 — An Environment For Success

before I went to school. That means I usually arose at about 4:00 a.m., took my lantern, and put on my boots, gloves, and warm hat. Then I took off across the country side on Back Creek to see if I had caught any animal in my traps. It was my dad's job to skin the animal and put the pelt on a board to dry before I took it to sell at a local store in Mount Eden. The kind of skin and its condition determined the price.

It was in the midst of these hard times that the Mount Moriah Baptist Church held a revival that brought the fire of God down on the little town of Mount Eden. The evangelist made it plain. Heaven was for the saved, hell was hot and it was for the unsaved. You had to make the decision which you wanted! It was 1942 and America was at war where American boys were spilling their blood for American freedom. I fell out with Sin and fell in Love with Jesus right quick. I walked down to that front seat and have never regretted it. I gave it all to Jesus that night. The Great Depression caused a lot of Americans to take a look at themselves. My father, for instance, was a church member but not saved.

Reverend Foster E. Howard was called to pastor at Mount Moriah Baptist Church during this difficult time, even though the church could not pay his salary. He got a job working on the dairy barn that was being constructed on our farm in the area. My dad was working on the same dairy barn. Through the friendship that developed over that period of time, my dad was soundly converted and baptized in the Mount Moriah Baptist Church.

My entire family is now converted. My sister Virginia Louise, who had been converted in a big revival that shook the entire community a few years earlier, is active in the Mount Moriah Baptist Church youth organizations, young women's activities, drama, choir, and training activities.

My mother and father are now the first people to get to church on Sunday morning and Sunday night. They are one hundred percent committed to Almighty God. (See Corinthians 6:20 and Matthew 6:33).

For more than twenty years my parents never missed a Sunday being in Sunday School. (See 2 Timothy 2:15).

God had chosen them for a special place in His Kingdom. He brought them out of poverty and sickness and set them on a solid rock. He took them places they never dreamed of and He let them see things their neighbors never saw. He allowed them to feel in their hearts a joy no man could place there. They had a story to tell that thrilled the world. Even in their final days on planet earth, their God kept His promise as recorded in Romans 8:26.

Chapter 3
College Doors Open

By the spring of 1945 the Great Depression years were now only memories for our family and my father was able to purchase the farm that at one time belonged to Frank Casey, my uncle. My father bought it from John Cosby, who had made many improvements to the farm. Over the next few years my father was able to buy my mother a refrigerator, a freezer, a washing machine, a radio, and a television. My father was able to purchase a tractor, a mower, plows, and many more new tools around the farm. I can only say, "Praise the Lord for staying so close to His Word."

In 1948 I graduated from the Mount Eden High School. What I should do with my life was resting heavily on my shoulders. The sun was shining bright in Kentucky and God was dealing with this country boy. I knew in my heart God was calling me to preach His Word, but I did not want to do that in this wicked world. However, after more than three years of running from the Lord, on June 10, 1951, I went forward in the Mount Moriah Baptist Church in Mount Eden and publicly announced to the church that I was surrendering my life to God to preach the Gospel. Shortly thereafter the church licensed me to preach the Gospel Ministry. As soon as I could, I enrolled at Georgetown College, Georgetown, Kentucky, to prepare for God's work.

My father and mother accepted the Bible as the Word of Almighty God and believed it was what people should follow. They felt that God's Word was what held the family together. There always seemed to be a bond in the Casey family that held it together no matter what happened along life's way. The precious truth that Christ lives in our lives as Christians was drilled in my heart during those years and has enabled me to rebuke sin in later experiences. My parents were behind me in the decision to be God's preacher man but there were those around who thought that the boy from Back Creek would not hold out. Some remembered when he was just a small child, he was a stutterer and stumbled over some words. Some murmured he hadn't done any public speaking while still others predicted he wouldn't last very long. With all of these negative things being circulated, the boy from Back Creek knew if anything good came out of his life, it would have to be the work of Almighty God.

September 1951 soon rolled around and my mother helped pack my suitcase for college. I could sense she was proud of me, yet at the same time there was going to be an empty place at the house. As I left the barn, I saw in my father a feeling of a lonely traveler.

When we got to Georgetown College and drove to the entrance of Pawling Hall, where I was going to room, they knew it was parting but indeed it was just the beginning of a great cause. My mother scaled the steps to the third floor where I would be staying in Room #318. She made the bed for me

Chapter 3 — College Doors Open

and looked out the window to see the good view and made a few comments as we both went down stairs where my dad was waiting. Soon they said goodbye and drove away.

I found myself with a host of other young preacher boys from all across America. It was not long until I met a young ministerial student named James Carpenter from Lynch, Kentucky. Looking back now I am sure God planned this meeting and I felt assured that God was pleased our paths had crossed. Jim was excited because he and a number of other students were in the process of starting a new mission on Main Street in Georgetown. He asked me to join them because they needed me. What Jim was talking about seemed to fit what God had called me to do. I remembered that I had filled out a form at the Admitting Office saying I wanted to be a Baptist evangelist and major in Bible. I took my place here at this store–front mission on Main Street and never turned back. It was my heart beat. It was dealing with people who others had passed by and who needed the Saviour too.

However, I was a poor boy myself and I needed a job to help me get through college. I asked the Admitting Office about applying for a job on the college campus and they suggested I might be able to get a job washing dishes at the college cafeteria for forty–five cents an hour. This sounded good for the boy from Back Creek. It all worked out as I was hired and worked about fifteen to twenty hours a week. It was fun for there were several of us boys who were engaged in the job and we laughed and talked and played jokes on one another as we worked. In time our work crew formed a bond and stuck together.

That first semester at Georgetown College was very difficult for the boy from Back Creek. Graduating from a small rural high school which offered very few college–prep courses left me ill–prepared to begin college level courses. I was thrown into classes with students from large schools in some of the largest cities in Kentucky and other states as Georgetown was the only Baptist four–year college in the state of Kentucky at that time. Well, I was out classed so there was only one way for me to meet this formidable challenge and that was to keep trusting Almighty God. In the middle of all this, one day I went to my college assigned post office box to find a letter from the Dean of the College.

I did not open it until I was alone in room 318 in Pawling Hall where I roomed and lived on campus. When I opened the letter, the words stunned me. It read, "Mr. Casey, you are not passing any of your subjects except Physical Education and this college does not allow any student to remain here who does not earn at least an average grade of C. Unless your grades improve, you will be dismissed from this institution at the end of the semester."

I began to cry like a baby. I did not want to go back home. I could not return to Back Creek. God had called me to preach. I confessed my sins to God. I pleaded to God for my forgiveness. I read the Bible meditating over and over on Matthew, Chapter 6:33–34 and then Chapter 7:7–11. I knew

Chapter 3 — College Doors Open

God was my Heavenly Father. My mother had drilled that into me ever since she enrolled me in the Cradle Roll. Suddenly, Psalm 46:1 came to me, "God is our refuge and strength, a very present help in trouble." I was in real trouble! I prayed, "O God, I'll do whatever it takes to get these grades up. I will not turn against you because I am here as God's boy from Back Creek and I am not going back home." It seemed that the curtains in the room ruffled and a breath of fresh air flowed through that room and I got up carrying a sword. I went to every class with a smile on my face and a thrill in my heart. God had breathed a breath of fresh air into the heart of the boy from Back Creek.

Chapter 4
Secrets To Success

It wasn't but a few weeks later and Thanksgiving Holidays came. I went home to see my mother and father for the first time since enrolling in Georgetown College. It was good to be home for a few days to see my parents and visit my home church but my heart was set on the mission work at Georgetown and on the class work God had called me to do. My mother washed all of my dirty clothes and arranged things so I could get back to Georgetown by sundown on Sunday evening. My tedious route was a challenge. My father took me to Shelbyville where I caught a bus going to Frankfort. There was no bus route into Georgetown so I got off with my luggage and stood by the road to hitch a ride the rest of the way. I waited there no more than ten minutes when a good minister going to Georgetown stopped and took me the rest of the way. God takes care of his own.

The first semester would be over about the middle of January. I was really studying hard. I was doing my best. My heart was in it. I was taking two Bible courses. I was going to major in Bible and minor in History. There was a war going on in my life. The devil was doing his best to knock me out. However, I knew God had called me and I was not going to back down! My calling was directly from God and He promised, "If you will take care of My business, I will take care of you." It was just that simple! It meant if I was doing God's Will, then wherever I was, God would take care of me.

So here I was working at my job washing dishes in the college cafeteria, ministering in the Main Street Baptist Mission, and taking a full load of college subjects that were really difficult for a Freshman. I was trying to be God's little boy from Back Creek. Would I fizzle out? Would God come on the scene and show His colors like He did with the boy David? Would He intervene for me like He did for Gideon? What about Joshua and the sun standing still? Has God Changed? But I read Malachi 3:6 where God says, "For I am the Lord, I change not."

Some students were now already laughing at the boy from Back Creek because he had been so outspoken about his faith in Almighty God. Exam time came and I went into every class with deep confidence that my God was watching over His Preacher Boy. When the first semester grades were released, I learned I had passed every subject!

All the things that were currently happening in my life were reminding me of what I was being taught in class by Dr. C. R. Daley, my Old Testament teacher at Georgetown College. We were studying the journey of the Israelites as they traveled out of Egypt. There they stood hemmed in on all sides as they met the Red Sea in front and daunting mountains on one side, the desert on the other. Behind was the pursuing Egyptian Army. As he looked at his students, Dr. Daley explained that there would be trials through our college life. He continued that God is often testing us to see if our faith is really genuine. Just as God opened the Red Sea for the Israelites to march through, I believe He opened up things at Georgetown so I could march to victory. God seemed to put in me a fearless boldness and I could say like David, "Yea, though I walk through the valley of the shadow of death, I will fear no evil" (Psalm 23:4). I just had a boldness as expressed in Psalm 118:6, "The Lord is on my side; I will not fear what man can do unto me."

Chapter 5

The Mission Field Beckons

Now I was ready for the second semester in Georgetown. I knew in my heart there was no turning back for the boy from Back Creek. With God's hand in my heart, I was determined to do His will and be God's evangelist. I took more Bible subjects to deepen my love for God and His Word. My longing to preach and witness was showing up at the Main Street Baptist Mission. I was doing street preaching, witnessing in the jail ministry, and going to the hospital to see the sick. I was helping with Bible teaching on Sunday nights and Wednesday evenings. The second semester of my freshman year seemed to fly by and I passed every course. I was thrilled that now I could enroll in the fall of 1952 as a full sophomore.

The summer of 1952 was filled with work on the farm with my parents who were excited that I could come home and help. In fact they agreed to give me a good interest in the farming if I would help with the crops during the summers and autumn school holidays. It turned out to be a good deal for the family. I was with them and grew to love and appreciate my parents more and more after being away at college.

As I returned to college in September of 1952 as a Sophomore, my focus converged on the mission work on Main Street. Some of those who had been working there did not return so that left a gap to be filled and I soon stepped in as a full time leader. I already carried a full load of studies at the college plus worked in the College cafeteria to help pay my way through. I noticed that the Mission was drawing the attention of more students as they enrolled at the college. This was good because it could be a training ground for students who were entering the field of Religious Ministry.

When we had such notable students like Evangelist Homer Martinez who was set to graduate in the spring of 1953, we would usually pack the building with students. Everyone loved Homer and his ability to communicate the Gospel Message to everyone regardless of age, creed, or color.

I introduced many young women to the Mission and used their musical talents, such as singing and playing musical instruments, in our programs. We provided the opportunity for numerous students to gain experience in leading singing on Saturday and Wednesday nights.

One day in March of 1953 my father and mother wrote me a wonderful letter. It said that as a result of my helping with the farm work, as agreed upon, my father had been able to purchase a 1951 two–door Chevrolet for me. In fact the car was sitting in front of their house, ready for me to pick up. I did not have a driver's license at that time so I enlisted one of my friends from Shelby County, who was also enrolled at Georgetown and had a license, to help me get the car. We hitch–hiked all the way from Georgetown to my home in Mount Eden. My friend drove the car to Georgetown for me. However, I was not long in getting my own driver's license. It

Chapter 5 — The Mission Field Beckons

was noticed now that the boy from Back Creek was one of the few on campus who had his own car.

It was also about this time that I moved out of Pawling Hall to room with my good friend James Carpenter, in a house owned by James Fisher. We found this less expensive than paying both our rents to the college. Since our house was just across the road from where we roomed, we continued to enjoy easy access to the College's activities.

I came to the end of my sophomore year with great joy in my heart. God was in full control and I was thrilled to be God's Man. I went home ready to do whatever God had in store for me. I had not been home very long and was working around the farm for only a few hours when the telephone rang.

Mother answered the phone and hastened to me to get on the line. The Mission had unanimously called me as pastor and wanted me to be on the field the very next Sunday. I turned to my father and mother, realizing they had expected me to farm all summer. In desperation I saw the dilemma, but my parents eased the path. My father urged me to return immediately to the Mission. He pleaded that this was the opportunity on which our hopes hinged. The work on the farm would get done somehow. And so I began to put my belongings in my suitcase, knowing all the time that this was the beginning of my life's work. I would never, no, never turn back. Before the sun had set, God's boy from Back Creek had said his farewell to farming forever—he had hitched his life to Almighty God wherever it led. I had put down the plow handle and was never looking back. The mission fields ahead beckoned.

Chapter 6
Giant Steps In Mission Work

I was glad to get back to Georgetown as a full time pastor at Main Street Baptist Mission and as a student at Georgetown College. The boy from Back Creek was now enrolling for his first time in summer school at the College and was completely satisfied. I took a full summer load and worked for the college as well. I was happy and the Holy Spirit seemed to be guiding me at full speed.

There were times when the College Administration gave me responsibilities such as go to the Post Office for mail, and then, distribute it at the college. At times I had in my possession a myriad of college keys. I'd scratch my head and ponder that such responsibilities were entrusted to me. Then I would whisper a Prayer of Thank You to the Father in Heaven.

I noticed in the summer school it was easier to get acquainted with the Faculty and College Leadership. The wife of one of the professors, who I dearly loved, stopped me on the campus and said she had a suit her son had outgrown. She would bring it the next day if I would like to accept it. I wore the suit for several years. Thanks to our Lord and His people who take care of things in His Kingdom.

The Mission was an exciting place to minister that summer and we had several people saved and I baptized my first converts that summer. We had some summer students who attended but our crowd was mostly from the local city. I did all the visitation I could and passed out many Gospel Tracts on the "Plan of Salvation". Many folks came as a result of getting the literature on their doorstep.

The summer seemed to pass rather quickly and since I was a full time pastor, I did not go home but remained on the field spending my time soul–winning. It did pay off as one young girl came forward and was wonderfully converted. The boy from Back Creek was having fun doing God's work in Georgetown. By September 4, 1953, I was twenty–three years old and ready to enroll in Georgetown College for the Junior Year. As I pondered on my life at this point, I fell on my knees in prayer to my Father in Heaven. God had been good to this little boy and I knew it. I dared not move to the right or the left. I wanted the blessings of the Father no matter what others said.

One day in the regular chapel service at the John L. Hill Chapel, I heard one of the Freshman girls sing, "I'd Rather Have Jesus." It so overwhelmed me that I could not rest until I met the singer. I wanted her to sing at the Main Street Baptist Mission some Sunday morning and I wanted to take her there. Indeed, I got to escort her to Sunday morning service and because of it we developed a great relationship which lasted a good while. She was a wonderful Christian girl and dedicated to the Lord. However, she thought I was too committed to some of my beliefs so we kindly went our ways in prayer and God's love. There were others who also thought I was somewhat too dedicated to my faith. However when I told

Chapter 6 — Giant Steps In Mission Work

them about my experience and that I could not turn back, they did not really know what to say.

It was at this point in my college life that Main Street Baptist Mission asked Georgetown Baptist Church to ordain me to the Gospel Ministry. The church scheduled the Ordination for October 18, 1953 at 3:00 p.m. and Dr. George Redding was to deliver the main message. I was glad that my mother and father could attend. Many of the college students came for the service and the Mission presented me with a copy of the Holy Bible.

I was glad to get the ordination behind me so that I could now march on to other things. There was so much I wanted to accomplish as a Minister of the Gospel. I had my mind in gear to get out of college as fast as I could. I was now thinking I possibly could get out in the summer of 1954, if all went well. That would mean I would graduate in three years. Could the boy from Back Creek do this? I was confident that with God all things are possible. It says in Genesis 18:14, "Is any thing too hard for the Lord?" I just couldn't get away from God's Word. Folks might laugh at me, but I knew if I clung to my beliefs in God's Word I would come out a winner.

Now that I was a full–time pastor and had full–time services each Sunday, I did not work in the college cafeteria on the weekend. I still worked in the dishwasher area during the weekdays to make money. The Mission paid me only seventy–five dollars a month for my services. The money was minimal but I was not in it for the money anyway. I was glad to be one of God's preacher boys delivering His word the best way I could.

I enjoyed my first Christmas as Pastor of the Main Street Baptist Mission but in my heart there was that longing to push on and on. I wanted to see what really could be accomplished.

When the second semester of my third year began, my eyes were focused on getting that Bachelor of Arts degree by the end of summer school. I saw where it was possible if I wanted to do it. God had opened the door and now it was left up to me to make the move.

Even when God opens a door it doesn't always mean it is easy. We had just finished studying in the Old Testament about how it wasn't easy capturing the Promised Land. I knew it wasn't going to be an easy road, but I knew it was a road that my God and I could handle. To attain my goal, I took twenty-two hours for the last semester. That was a big load, but God told me, "If you will take care of my business, I will take care of you." So now it was in God's hands and He would never let one of His servants down. When you know that you are in the Divine Will of Almighty God, things move along so smoothly. The last semester went by without any problems.

I preached with power and the fullness of the Holy Spirit in every service and my grades were all improving. I never once had any worries. It was so amazing that semester. Many students wondered how I could take twenty-two hours and still keep my grades up. I would often reply, "It's all by faith."

Chapter 6 — Giant Steps In Mission Work

Now, if certain courses were going to be offered for the summer I would be able to get my degree and meet my goal of graduating by the end of summer. Would God come on the scene with the schedule I needed? The summer schedule was finally posted. I was not at all surprised when I saw that all the classes I needed were going to be offered. I would be able to graduate on August 13, 1954.

I have found out that God knows how to arrange things better than I do if I am willing to let Him do it. So all I did was just sign–up for the Summer Program and every thing worked out. I took my last course in French and wonder of wonders I made the best grade I had ever made in French. Praise the Lord! PRAISE THE LORD!

Chapter 7

New Ministry In The Mountains

At this time the Holy Spirit was dealing intensely with me about my life's work. I did not want to settle down because God had called me to be a Baptist Evangelist, but now it looked like I was going to be involved in Mission work.

Only recently at a Georgetown College Chapel program, Dr. Eldred M. Taylor, of the Mission program of the General Association of Baptists in Kentucky (now the Kentucky Baptist Convention), had challenged the student body to come into the mountains of Eastern Kentucky. Eastern Kentucky was a field ready to be harvested. His challenge was still ringing in my ears, in my mind, and in my heart so that I could not shake it off. Some how it seemed as if God was urging me to respond to this challenge.

I remembered when the boy Samuel lay upon his pillow in the stillness of the night and God called him. As soon as Samuel realized that God was calling he replied, "Speak; for thy servant heareth" (1 Samuel 3:10). So one night I told the Lord I would write to Dr. Eldred M. Taylor and tell him I would be ready to go as soon as I graduated from Georgetown College. I wrote to Dr. Taylor as I promised and he forwarded the information on to Rev. John R. Isaacs, the Associational Missionary of Pine Mountain Association in Fleming, Kentucky. Rev. John R. Isaacs promptly sent a letter to me saying that the McRoberts Baptist Church in McRoberts was in need of a pastor. He made arrangements for me to go there as a prospective pastor and as a Missionary of the General Association of Baptists in Kentucky. There were several men at the summer school that year from Eastern Kentucky and I shared with them my plans to go to McRoberts, in Letcher County, to preach, and perhaps eventually serve as a Missionary Pastor. God always has a way of putting things together. The key is God has a plan if you will seek to fit into it.

There was a school teacher/preacher in need of a ride home after school. He lived in Beattyville, which is about half way to McRoberts and on the exact road I would be traveling. McRoberts is almost on the Virginia State line. I gave him a ride home and told him I would pick him up on the way back to Georgetown.

Another fellow student, a school teacher, who would graduate with me in August, joined in our trip. He lived in Neon, which is less then four miles south of McRoberts. The journey from Georgetown to McRoberts was about two hundred fifty miles.

In His divine plan God had provided these traveling companions as they were excellent teachers for me during the long commute between our homes and college. If God has His hand on you He will lead you.

I had never been this far east in the Appalachian mountains before this trip. I was excited about being in McRoberts, a coal mining town. Just about everything in these small coal mining

Chapter 7 — New Ministry In The Mountains

towns was owned by the coal mining company. In McRoberts, it was the Consolidation Coal Company. The church had made arrangements for me to stay at the Company Club House, on the corner of Chopping Branch and Cannel City Row, which was just across the street from the Company Store. With the gracious spirit of the people of McRoberts, I was a very enthusiastic twenty–three–year–old preacher.

The building where I was staying was used as a guest house by the Company and was also made available to others in need. It was constructed of wood and had a large front porch with several chairs for relaxation. The room I stayed in was very comfortable and I enjoyed it very much. I went to bed that night and asked God for a clear vision on what to preach and how to go about it in this coal mining town. God let me know that I should be the boy from Back Creek and that He would take care of the rest.

On Sunday morning, I opened up God's Word the best way I knew how and told the congregation about Jesus and how to get saved. I told them that's what the Cross was all about. My preaching must have pleased the Heavenly Father and the people, because they all listened closely and I enjoyed the experience.

On the way back to Georgetown I picked up the two school teachers as planned. They inquired about my experience in McRoberts. I told them that I really enjoyed it and that it now rested in God's hands and the people of McRoberts.

A few days later Bro. Isaacs wrote me a letter saying the Church wanted me as their pastor. He gave me a description of the General Association of Baptists and my potential position there as a Missionary. He asked me to pray about living in the mountains and serving the Lord there. Bro. Isaacs wanted me to reply very soon and hoped I would say, "Yes." I wrote back shortly and stated that as soon as I graduated I wanted a few days off and that I would be there September 1, 1954.

My heart was now fixed. The word was all over Georgetown that Jim Casey was going to the mountains to preach. People asked lots of questions. One professor asked if I was afraid since he heard the folks in that area were dangerous. I assured him that if God could take care of David in front of a giant, He could take care of me. He concluded that I had a lot of faith.

I presented my resignation as Pastor of the Main Street Baptist Mission, effective the last Sunday in August 1954. During my tenure I had lead the Mission in a Relocation Project so we could own our building. A site was purchased on Royal Springs Street and dedicated to the Glory of God on August 2, 1954. Dr. George Redding preached the dedication message.

It was Friday, August 13, 1954, the day for the Annual Summer School Commencement Service at Georgetown College when twenty-eight students would receive their degrees. Graduates were having their pictures taken, families were gathering, friends were arriving from all directions. Dr.

Chapter 7 — New Ministry In The Mountains

John R. Carter, president of Campbellsville College in Kentucky, was delivering the main address. My parents were in the audience and I was proud of them, realizing that much of this journey belonged to them.

When the commencement was over we said our goodbyes and my parents went home. It had been a long day and the time finally arrived to go to that earthly place where we catch our sleep; that's when soul searching rises from our being. Suddenly scenes flew across my mind—three years at Georgetown College were gone — so I cried a little, I laughed. You see I was alone in my room, just God and me.

The people of Georgetown had been good to me. When I went to the Financial Office of the college to check out, I was told that not only were all my bills paid, but that they had a check for me. I had worked at the college until graduation and was given my last paycheck. So I walked away from Georgetown College with a B.A. degree and did not owe anyone a single penny.

Chapter 8
Mission In A Coal Mining Town

I will never forget when J. C. Penny came to Georgetown College to speak to the student body. I sat there and listened to every word. He told how he saved money and how at one time he lost it all. He had to start over again. J. C. Penny told the student body to never leave God out of their lives. J. C. Penny was faithful in giving his tithes even in hard times as well as in good times. I applied what J. C. Penny said to my life that summer and it worked. It was sometimes hard to follow, but our Lord never did tell us that life would be a bed of roses. "God is our refuge and strength, an ever-present help in trouble" (Psalm 46:1 NIV).

The Main Street Baptist Mission and the Georgetown Baptist Church were given notice that I was graduating from Georgetown College and would be leaving my position as Pastor of the Main Street Baptist Mission effective Sunday, August 29, 1954, following the evening service.

It was difficult to leave a place in which you had worked since its beginnings, but I realized I must march on to other things to do God's work. I had witnessed so much there in that little Mission setting. I had witnessed in jail, preached on the street corner, and ministered to sick people at the local hospital. I had stood by several families at the grave sites but most of all I saw the rejoicing when someone came to know Jesus as their Saviour and this rejoicing always reminded of those words in the Scripture "Rejoice with me; for I have found my sheep which was lost" (Luke 15:6).

A young freshman girl at Georgetown College became very attached to me. This was not the first time that happened. Girls seem to look for boys who know where they are going. Girls really want a boy who means business in life. When I started college, I did not study to become a preacher but God called me from the plow handle in Shelby County. I simply went to college to sharpen my mind so I could do a better job at what God had already called me to do. So when girls got around me, and they did, they found a fellow who was able to explain where he was heading.

This little freshman girl, perhaps because she was younger than I, hung on for the ride. It was exciting and I guess we both learned something from days of togetherness at the Mission. When she found out about my decision to go to McRoberts as pastor she sought me out. She wanted to tell me that she had relatives in Neon, a small town near McRoberts. She also told me that her father was a coal miner and he worked in a coal mine at Leatherwood, which is also near McRoberts. So I offered this girl a ride from Georgetown College to Neon to see her relatives.

I packed all of my books, which by this time constituted my growing library because many books were given to me at Georgetown. I also had several boxes of clothes, college notes, and other things. Of course all of this went with me in my black two–door 1951 Chevrolet.

Chapter 8

Mission In A Coal Mining Town

By the time I got all of my boxes and all the girl's suitcases loaded, the little car was full. We had a prayer of thanksgiving for our years of college work and ministry at Georgetown, and then we headed for the mountains of Eastern Kentucky, about a 250 mile trip. She provided directions as I drove through towns like Frenchburg, West Liberty, Salyersville, Paintsville, Prestonburg, Pikeville, Jenkins, and finally Neon. I escorted her up the side of the mountain where her relatives lived. I continued on to McRoberts. I finally reached my destination, the town I came to pastor.

I drove up to Mr. R. P. Narramore's home where I had been a guest for lunch when I spoke in the church in my previous visits. It was getting late in the day and the sun was going over the mountains and I whispered a prayer of thanksgiving to God for the safe trip.

When I knocked on the door Mr. Narramore came to the door and said, "What are you doing here?"

I said, "I came to pastor the church."

He fired back, "They have laid off 200 men in the coal mines here and we can't pay your salary."

With a smile I beamed, "I am here to stay and I am not going any place else."

He reasoned, "If you are that kind of a person, let me see what I can do to get you a place to live." Then he declared, "Rev. John Isaacs at Fleming might be able to house you for a few days until we can do something."

He phoned Rev. John Isaacs and I drove to his house in Fleming, where I stayed with him and his wife Lillian and their small child for several days. As I drove along I remembered the words of the Psalmist, "O thou that hearest prayer" (Psalm 65:2).

Rev. John Isaacs and his family came to understand me better and I learned of his heartbeat for God and the mountain mission work.

A call soon came to the home of Rev. Isaacs that the church had rented a nice little house for me and it was ready. The house was just across from the McRoberts Baptist Church. It was a little three–room house nestled upon the side of the mountain. It was complete with a stove, refrigerator, bed, gas heating stove, table, and anything else I needed.

It was now Saturday night and I knew in my heart that the people in McRoberts would come out tomorrow to hear this young man preach and I must give my very best. I leaned on the Psalmist verse, "I will lift up my eyes unto the hills, from whence cometh my help. My help cometh from the Lord, which made heaven and earth" (Psalm 121:1–2).

It was Sunday, September 5, 1954, just one day after my twenty–fourth birthday. I was single, a missionary, and a full–time pastor. I hit the pulpit filled with the SPIRIT OF ALMIGHTY GOD and it seemed like Heaven came down and kissed the earth that day. We had a great time in both services at God's blessed house of worship. The people were pleasant and friendly. I ate in someone's home for lunch and talked to

Chapter 8 — Mission In A Coal Mining Town

the folks about coal mining, public schools and other mutual interests.

Eventually, I started going from house to house in McRoberts telling folks about the Lord Jesus Christ and passing out Gospel tracts. I wanted the people to understand that I loved them and that God loved them and that no matter what they had done in life, it was possible to get forgiveness.

I attended the PTA meetings in the grade school and took part in the community activities. The high school boys and girls were transported by bus from McRoberts to Jenkins High School because they were part of that school system. Several times when a school teacher was sick, or for some reason was absent, I was substituting teacher at Jenkins High School. I won the hearts of a lot of boys and girls and got them to go to McRoberts Baptist Church. However, it was not all fun as many endured the suffering. I was at the hospital often. I presided over several funerals of dear ones who were struck down suddenly, others after periods of sickness, some taken in youth, and even a small baby.

One of the interesting things I did was visit one–room schools that were out in rural Letcher County. I would either speak to the children, show slide pictures, or show a 16mm movie. At first I got the equipment from the local library but later I got my own equipment and I showed materials from Billy Graham and his organization. As far as I know, I was the only person in the mountains doing this kind of mission ministry. Some of these one–room schools were way back on the country roads and had only a few students, but it met a need and God knew they needed to hear about Jesus.

Chapter 9
Comfortable Only For A While

The Consolidated Coal Company was in charge of the Company Store in McRoberts. The Company Store sold just about everything that you would need or want. They had clothing, groceries, jewelry, furniture, appliances, and much more. They even sold gasoline. The Company Store still used scrip, which was a type of currency used by the Company to pay their workers and could only be used in the Company Store. Paying the coal miners with scrip forced a lot of the coal miners to trade exclusively at the Company Store.

Not long after arriving, the McRoberts Baptist Church gave me a pounding—a tradition in the mountains where the church members would welcome their new pastor by bringing a pound of food. The church was very generous at Christmas too. This was something a twenty-four-year-old pastor never dreamed would happen. These people had taken me in when I had no place to go and I had given them my best. God's word resonated in my mind, "He will not forsake thee" (Deuteronomy 4:31). I found it true. Psalm 105:42 says, "For He remembered His holy promise, and Abraham his servant." Now God remembered me, His servant.

The Fleming Baptist Church, another church just down the road in Fleming, was having some pastoral problems. Rev. John R. Isaacs discussed the problems with me and asked me if I would be willing to help for a little while until things improved. This was brought before the McRoberts Baptist Church as well as the State Mission Board of the General Association of Baptists in Kentucky to see if all were agreeable. It was common knowledge all over the area that I was working twelve to sixteen hours every day, I had no ties because I was single, I was full of the Spirit and I preached Hell Fire and Damnation without fear. I interacted with all the other church denominations in the area and I treated everyone the same no matter whether they had only a dime or drove a Cadillac.

After much discussion and all sides agreeing, I accepted the position as pastor at Fleming Baptist Church in addition to remaining as pastor at McRoberts Baptist Church. Since the Fleming pastor had left, the parsonage was available and I moved in there. It was located in the back part of the church. It was a very convenient deal, especially for a young, single preacher. It was very nice and comfortable. In 1 Kings 12:24 it says, "…return every man to his house; for this thing is from me." No person could have made this happen; it was the work of Almighty God.

On Sundays I would begin the day by preaching first at Fleming Baptist Church at 9:45 a.m., while McRoberts Baptist Church was having Sunday School. Then I would drive 1 1/2 miles to McRoberts and have the worship service there at 11:00 a.m., while they were having Sunday School in Fleming. I did not always preach the same sermon at both churches. God knows different people need different things. I would ask God

Chapter 9 Comfortable Only For A While

to give me what he wanted me to preach at both places. I would go back to Fleming on Sunday evenings to hold worship service at 6:30 p.m. Then I would drive back to McRoberts and have worship service there at 7:45 p.m. Mid–week service was held on Wednesday nights at McRoberts and on Thursday nights at Fleming.

I also starting writing a weekly article for the Letcher County newspaper, *The Mountain Eagle*. It was composed of about one thousand words each week and I would tell about church related activities going on in the community. When Summer came around we had Vacation Bible School at both Churches, which was a blessing to the community. We had boys and girls coming who had no Bible or New Testament. We were able to put a copy in their hands. Later many of those boys and girls were won to Jesus Christ. Sometimes the entire family was saved.

This area in the mountains of Kentucky was segregated, black and whites, just like most of the country. I did not let that hinder me. I recall going up to a black Baptist Church in McRoberts and taking part in their worship services when they had revivals or needed a guest speaker. In turn, we invited members of the black Baptist Church to take part in the services at McRoberts Baptist Church.

One of our dear men in the community who was loved by all, suddenly died and his funeral was held at the Free Will Baptist Church in McRoberts. I got to the church a little early and was outside talking with some of the men when the

Undertaker came up to me and asked if I was Rev. Casey. I told the man I was and that I came to show my support for the family. He told me the pastor of the Free Will Baptist Church had to work and was not going to be able to make it to the service. He asked me if I would be willing to take over the service. I told him that if it was alright with the family I would be glad to perform the service. I went forward and opened God's word and preached about how God loved us so much that He gave His only Son to save us from a Devil's Hell. I was informed that this man who had passed on was wonderfully saved. So I closed the service by quoting John 3:16, "…that whosoever believeth in him should not perish, but have everlasting life."

Chapter 10
A Girl Keeps Reappearing

One of the interesting things about being a single pastor is that the mothers in the churches are always anxious to introduce you to their daughters. Of course they did not understand that I had made a promise to God that I would not date any girl on my church field. However, it was good fellowship and the sweetness of the event was wonderful.

In 1955 as a missionary of the General Association of Baptists in Kentucky, I had opportunities to go to Ridgecrest in North Carolina, Cedarmore Baptist Assembly in Kentucky, and to Oneida Baptist Institute in Oneida, Kentucky. I had been to all of these churches this calendar year. I was doing so much driving over the mountain roads that my little 1951 Chevrolet was about to give up on me. I had a friend in Fleming who was a car salesman for the Ford dealer in Hazard. I got a great deal on a new 1955 Ford Fairlane.

However, the Home Mission Board of the Southern Baptist Convention at Atlanta, Georgia, came knocking at my door. I was asked to be one of the speakers at a Schools Of Missions program in Blytheville, Arkansas. I thought to myself, "How could a twenty–five–year–old boy from Back Creek be a speaker at a Schools of Missions?" I felt like David when he was a young boy and he went to fight the the giant, Goliath. He had no experience in war and yet he could handle a nine–foot–tall giant. God was throwing me into this group of learned preachers, missionaries, and teachers for a purpose. God had a purpose for David being in a battle and I believe God had a purpose for me going on this mission trip to Arkansas. I did not want to question what God was trying to do in my life. I simply said, "Here I am Lord, send me."

The Rev. W. L. Crumpler, pastor of the Central Baptist Church in Maysville, Kentucky, wrote me a letter saying he was driving his car to Blytheville. He said he was coming by Ravenna, Kentucky, to pick up Rev. Arlan Davis and I could join them on the trip to Arkansas. I drove to Ravenna on December 3, 1955, and all three of us headed west for Blytheville, Arkansas. I rode in the back seat and did a little talking but I listened to every word of these two senior preachers because I wanted to know more about Kingdom work and how to do it.

After we had driven many miles Rev. Crumpler asked me if I had a wife. I simply told him I was still looking around. As quick as a bolt of lightning he said, "I've got the girl for you in my church." He started describing her and every few minutes he would look back at me and say, "You've got to see this girl!" He kept telling me that this girl was the girl for me. All the time I was praying we would soon get to Blytheville and this playful bedeviling would be over. I was starting to get uncomfortable.

When we finally got to Blytheville we all went in different directions and I was very glad and relieved. This was my first experience being out like this and I was enjoying it very much.

Chapter 10 — A Girl Keeps Reappearing

I was inexperienced and perhaps my presentation was not like some of the other speakers. I simply spoke about Jesus. I told them what He had done for me and what He was doing in the little churches God had entrusted into my hands.

The three of us started back home. Somewhere out on the highway the Lord had Rev. Crumpler bring up the subject of that beautiful girl from his church. He told me her name was Oleta Lancaster and that I just had to meet her. It was right then and there I decided I was willing to meet this girl. I asked Rev. Crumpler how I was going to meet this wonderful girl from his church. He said, "That's a real good question."

After thinking on it for a while, he told me that in April his Association was holding a Schools of Missions and if I could be one of the speakers then I would have an opportunity to meet this incredible girl he kept going on about. I told him I would check my calendar when I got back home. Once we got back to our perspective homes we continued to correspond with each other. It worked out with my schedule in April so I agreed to be one of the speakers at the Schools of Missions. We both coordinated our calendars and the plan was set in motion. He said in one of his letters that I would find Oleta in the church basement at 2:00 p.m. folding church bulletins.

Back in Fleming and McRoberts I plunged into work that was in dire need. The Christmas season was soon upon us and we had to work hard to get things done. We delivered food baskets to several families and gave toys and gifts to a lot of children in the community. I continued to do hospital visitations as well as home visitations to win the lost in the community.

The Fleming Hospital was run by Dr. Scaggs, a well established doctor who had been in Fleming for a good number of years. I had the privilege of baptizing Dr. Scaggs and his daughter in the presence of his wife, who was already a Christian and member at Fleming.

The Fleming Baptist Church tried to start a new mission in the Hemp Hill area using the grade school ministry to begin the work. This undertaking had been an extra strain on me. I had to prepare for and preside over five services every Sunday. I had two services, morning and evening, at each of the churches, Fleming and McRoberts, and one service at the new mission at 2:00 p.m. However, the mission did not work as desired and so the mission endeavor was discontinued.

Time soon passed and April came around. I found myself at the Missions Program in Maysville. I was anxious to see this beautiful girl who Rev. Crumpler described and talked about so much. When I went to the Central Baptist Church I found Oleta in the basement folding bulletins just as he had told me. She was as sweet looking as he had described and I really believe a little bit more. Our first conversation focused on usual Christian news. It was nice to see that she was committed to hard work.

As the week went along, I visited Oleta at her home, 531 Pelham Street, several times. I remember speaking with her mother, Iva, and her younger sister, Daisy. The family

Chapter 10 — A Girl Keeps Reappearing

displayed a tight bond and family unity. I appreciated that family's love for one another. I returned to Fleming and McRoberts with the feeling in my heart that here was a young lady who was brought up right. She was mature in her thinking, she displayed her love for the Kingdom, and she was not ashamed of her testimony.

Shortly after getting back to my home in Letcher County I wrote Oleta a letter indicating that I would enjoy hearing from her, if she cared to write. I closed the letter—

With Love and Prayers,
James

I mailed the letter to her on May 10, 1956, and I left it in the hands of God. I believed if God was in this He would bring it all together, just like He had brought me through college.

It was not long until Oleta wrote back and we began to correspond with each other. She was busy with her responsibilities and I was working hard at Fleming and McRoberts. Independence Day was coming up and I was looking forward to it, because I planned on visiting her in Maysville. We were able to see each other again and spend some quiet time together.

Chapter 11
Responding to God

As I moved about these two communities I realized I could not continue at this pace as pastor much longer or I would have a breakdown of some kind. I decided I would take a sabbatical leave and enroll for one semester at the Southern Baptist Theological Seminary in Louisville, Kentucky, beginning in September of 1956. I sent my resignation to both churches. My last service was set for August 26, 1956. It was a shock to some but others knew I could not continue at this pace much longer. Being a full–time pastor at two Baptist churches was really more than one person could handle over a long period of time.

Both churches gave me a going away party and it was a good celebration for everyone. When I started at McRoberts the average Sunday School attendance was fifty–eight and now they were averaging one hundred twenty–five. Their membership had grown from sixty to one hundred five members really dedicated to Jesus Christ. The youth were absolutely outstanding and I loved them dearly. I really hated to say farewell and tears came to my eyes as I drove away from there my last night.

During my tenure with the Fleming Baptist Church, I had seen twenty–five additions to the membership of the Church. Twenty–three were by baptism and two by letter of baptism. God had been good to us and His blessing had flowed upon us like a mighty stream of water. The people were always cooperative and many improvements were made on the property to the glory of Almighty God. It was hard for me to leave the mountains because I loved the people and they knew it. I was not there for the money, fame or glory, but because of a command of God. I never have forgotten my experiences there and I believe God wants me to remember them.

    I enrolled for the Fall term at Southern Baptist Theological Seminary and was accepted. I had not decided whether to stay with my parents at their house and commute to Louisville or to stay on campus. I pulled into my mother's and father's farm with my car loaded with all my earthly possessions. I decided I would try to stay on campus first and see how it worked out. I soon discovered that there were two preachers living in Mount Eden who were already commuting to the campus in Louisville. We discussed our schedules and now I was able to stay with my parents and commute to school with the others.

    I had not been at the Seminary very long when it was announced that Billy Graham was opening up his Greater Louisville Crusade in Freedom Hall at the Kentucky Fair Grounds in Louisville. There were various organizations having meetings across the city and of course the Seminary was deeply involved in the Crusade.

    One morning I had the wonderful opportunity to attend a breakfast and I met Dr. Mordecai F. Ham, of Louisville, Kentucky. He was an evangelist in 1934 at Charlotte, North Carolina, when a blond, sixteen-year-old boy called William Franklin Graham, Jr. was converted. I never will forget meeting him. One night a bus load of people from Maysville came to the Crusade. Oleta was on the bus and I was eagerly waiting to see her again. We sat together at the Crusade. It was so good to look into her face and see the love and commitment as Billy Graham preached God's word.

Chapter 12

Time For Life's Partner

I was trying to see Oleta every weekend. Quite often she would do some typing for me and that was a plus for me, because the professors wanted their students to keep notes and then turn them in at the end of the semester. I remember one Saturday night we sat in my car in front of her house and I tenderly asked her to be my wife. She was trembling but she said, "Yes, Jim." I could tell it was from her heart; she meant she would never turn back. Shortly after this I brought the ring and placed it on her finger. It wasn't long until she had set the wedding day, June 22, 1957.

Time was zipping by and my soul was aching to return to the mountains in Eastern Kentucky. I seemed to be rested and refreshed. I was more relaxed after getting out from under that tremendous load I was carrying seven days a week at the Seminary.

I contacted Rev. J. Edward Cunningham, director of the Mountain Mission Program of the General Association of Baptists in Kentucky. I told him of my desire to serve God in Eastern Kentucky. He sent me a letter telling me about the Phelps/Majestic Mission Field in Pike County, Kentucky. He said that the Home Mission Board was willing to assist with the project. I sent word to him that I would like to take on the mission field in Pike County. I told him I would be available the first week of February 1957.

I finished the semester at the Seminary about the middle of January 1957. I discussed all of my plans with Oleta. I told her about my calling from God to do His work and she seemed to understand. I knew this was going to be difficult for her but doing God's work is never guaranteed to be a life of ease. However, the same God who took care of Abraham, Isaac, and Jacob can take care of his servants today. Malachi 3:6 says, "For I am the Lord, I change not." I did not want Oleta to get into something that she would regret so we talked and prayed earnestly before we got married. I was at times quite sharp in discussing things because I was a seasoned soldier of the Cross and I knew what it was like.

The thing that I could never get very far from was that encounter I had with God and the Holy Spirit that first semester at Georgetown College. I told Oleta about God speaking to me, "If you will take care of My business, I will take care of you." God had kept His promise and I could not let my God down. Even though I had not seen it with my natural eyes, I felt that the door was opening up for Pike County. Like Abraham I was going on faith.

I began my journey in my 1955 Ford. On the way to Williamson, West Virginia, I ran into a winter snow and ice storm. I had an accident. I was alright but the car was badly damaged. I stopped in Hazard and traded my car in for a new black and white 1957 Ford. It was getting late and I noticed on the road map I could save time and many miles if I would take a gravel road and bypass several of the small towns. I took this

Chapter 12 — Time For Life's Partner

gravel road and within a few minutes some car lights flashed up behind me and a bunch of gangsters began to yell and flag me down. I let them pass me. I was thinking they would be somewhere down the road waiting for me. I had only driven a few miles and there they were standing along the side of the road. I said, "Lord, it's you and I and we are going to out run them." That is exactly what I did with God's help. Praise the Lord!

It was after midnight by the time I crossed the Tug River into Williamson, West Virginia. I had made it. I already had reservations at a motel there and that is where I spent the night. I thanked the Lord for safety and protection, and His deliverance from the hand of the evil ones along the roadway. I rested peacefully.

Sunday morning I was to go back into Kentucky to the Road Fork Baptist Church for the morning worship service. Their pastor was Rev. D. E. Meade. This morning they were observing the Lord's Supper and they had the table so beautifully set in the center of the building. Right at the opening of the service one of the deacons stood up and addressed the church body in a most business–like way and said, "We are delighted to have Rev. James Casey visiting with us today. I move that we admit Rev. Casey to the Lord's table."

Over on the other side of the building a well dressed deacon stood up and said, "I second the motion that Rev. Casey be admitted to the Lord's table."

The church body said, "Amen!"

The Boy From Back Creek

James E. Casey, Jr.

Chapter 13
A New Starting Point

I soon learned my way around the Phelps/Majestic mission area, thanks to Rev. D. E. Meade. From Williamson, West Virginia, I crossed the Tug River—known today as Tug Fork—into Pike County, Kentucky, where Freeburn, Majestic, Phelps, Jamboree and Coleman were all a part of this vast mission field. It was right on the state line of Virginia and West Virginia. After seeing the great need for Baptist work here, I committed my self to this mission field. The nearest Southern Baptist missionary was thirty-five to fifty miles away. It was fifty miles to Pikeville, the county seat of Pike County.

At this time the coal mines in the Freeburn and Majestic area were about all closed. Many of the miners were looking for jobs in other places. Unemployment was rather high in the surrounding communities.

Rev. Meade mentioned to me that just across the Tug River from Williamson was a small Baptist Church in Aflex, Kentucky, that needed a pastor. He said, "I don't see why you couldn't take that on as a beginning point." I immediately looked into the position as pastor of the Aflex Baptist Church. It was not long afterward that I was accepted as their pastor. Charles Gillespie and his family were members of the Aflex Baptist Church and they had a spare room in the attic where I stayed until I could find a rental house.

Things were really moving fast for me now. In addition to accepting the pastor position at Aflex, I notified Rev. J. Edward Cunningham that I was willing to take on the responsibilities of the Phelps/Majestic mission field in Pike County. The East Williamson Baptist Church in Williamson, West Virginia, would be the sponsoring church for the mission work in the Phelps/Majestic area.

At this time there was no State Baptist Convention in West Virginia. For that reason several Southern Baptist churches in West Virginia were affiliated with the Southern Baptists of Kentucky. It was very common for church members of East Williamson Baptist Church to come into Kentucky to do mission work and they were very happy to take on that responsibility. Rev. M. D. Wadley was the Pike County missionary. We had many discussions on my new assignment with him.

I stayed in Williamson, about thirty–five miles from Phelps, since I could not find suitable housing in Phelps. I was also finding it difficult to find a place to start a mission. I looked along the roads as I traveled but I could not find anything available. I would often leave Williamson right after day break with my brown bag lunch and bottle of water. I would not get home until the sun was setting. I had spent the day walking up hollow after hollow taking my house–to–house survey. The survey in the greater Phelps area revealed that there were about eight thousand people nestled in between those hollows and

Chapter 13 — A New Starting Point

mountains. Many of them did not know Jesus as their personal saviour.

While I was doing survey work, Oleta continued to write me. She would send me messages like "I am so glad the Lord saw fit to bring us together" and "You know I love you and long for your presence." Then she would quote Philippians 4:13 NKJV, "I can do all things through Christ who strengthens me." Letters like that from someone who loves you and is devoted to Almighty God touched and encouraged the very depths of my soul. I tried to keep Oleta informed on every detail going on in the mission field. I was honest and frank in telling her the conditions I faced and the conditions she would be facing. She would repeat over and over, "Honey, we'll just trust our God."

Meanwhile, the Aflex Baptist Church was now growing by leaps and bounds. They voted to use Southern Baptist Literature in their Sunday School classes. Mr. and Mrs. Guilford Jude, as well as several other members from the East Williamson Baptist Church, gave of their time, talents, and finances to help with the Aflex ministry. Mr. and Mrs. Jude had a gracious spirit offering me care, refuge, and meals in their home.

The youth in Aflex were also responding in such a remarkable way that the whole community seemed to rally behind what was happening at the Aflex Baptist Church. As a result of one of our revival meetings, I baptized eleven people on Sunday night, May 26, 1957. The East Williamson Baptist Church permitted us to use their Baptistry.

The General Association of Baptists in Kentucky sponsored this mission project and paid my salary. I was paid three hundred dollars monthly salary, fifty dollars monthly housing allowance, plus a retirement plan and medical insurance.

Chapter 14
The Wedding

Time was moving fast because Oleta and I had to plan for our up-coming wedding. I had some belongings at my parents' house so Mr. and Mrs. Guilford Jude agreed to let me use their trailer. We drove to my parents' house with the trailer. We filled the trailer and my car and delivered it to my house in Williamson, West Virginia. Meanwhile, Oleta wrote that the people at Central Baptist Church of Maysville had given her a wedding shower.

Oleta, her sister Daisy, and Mrs. Lancaster arrived as planned, the first week in June 1957. The wedding was only about three weeks away. I was glad to see them and welcomed them to the little brown house on the west side of Williamson, West Virginia. The day after Oleta arrived, we went to Pikeville, Kentucky, to get our blood tests and marriage license. The travel was a good introduction for Oleta to the mountains of Eastern Kentucky and West Virginia. After we got everything taken care of in Pikeville, the three women returned to their home in Maysville. I headed to the men's clothing store in Williamson and purchased a Navy blue suit for the wedding. It was complimented by a new tie and white shirt.

On June 8, 1957, I went to Phelps where I had scheduled a one-night service in the Phelps Court House building. There were six people in attendance and they said they were interested in starting a Baptist mission in Phelps. They agreed to make it a matter of prayer and we would convene after the wedding to discuss the possibility and the best place to begin. I told them Oleta and I would come to Phelps July 8–12 and that we would conduct a Vacation Bible School at the Phelps Court House building. I asked the people attending the mission services to go out and get as many children to attend as possible.

I was spending as much time as possible in the Majestic, Freeburn, and Phelps areas. I talked to teachers in all the schools I could get in and used every means possible to get the message out to the people. In Matewan, West Virginia, I stopped at a Christian radio station and asked them to advertise our ministry. I kept in mind my vision of a Baptist church which would not only preach the Gospel but also minister to the needs of the folks in the community. I wanted to feed the hungry, cloth the needy, and teach the children and youth about Jesus Christ.

It was now Friday, June 21, 1957, so I made sure everything was secure around the little brown house before I left for Maysville. I also spent some time in prayer and thanksgiving to the Father in Heaven for His goodness and mercy.

I made it to Maysville and was full of anticipation. I spent the night with Rev. and Mrs. Crumpler, as I did many times before when I came to see Oleta. I always enjoyed their

Chapter 14 — The Wedding

fellowship. I told them all about the mission work I had been involved in recently.

It was June 22, 1957, and the big day had finally arrived. Since I did not want my car to be bedecked with ribbons and streamers, I asked Rev. Crumpler to move my car to a safe place. He was always an understanding friend. Rev. W. L. Crumpler was the pastor of the Central Baptist Church and was the one who introduced Oleta and me to each other; it was only right that he officiate the wedding ceremony.

Saturday afternoon quickly arrived. I was truly glad to see that my parents made it to the church which was beautifully decorated. The organist filled the sanctuary with beautiful music. My parents were accompanied by my sister, Virginia Louise Newlen, and her husband, Charles Newlen, who was to be the best man at my wedding. Their young son, Scotty, was with them. They lived in Louisville, Kentucky.

As planned, Oleta did not want the boy from Back Creek to see his beautiful bride until the time of the wedding. She wanted to save the moment all for her Jim. There had been no wedding rehearsal, but Oleta and I were both ready. Since I was accustomed to standing up in front of people I had no problem facing the crowd. The boy from Back Creek walked out and stood at the front of the church in amazement as his beautiful bride walked slowly down the aisle. I was absolutely overwhelmed at her beauty—the fairest among ten thousand.

For the record, Oleta Frances Lancaster and I, James Elmo Casey, Jr., were married on June 22, 1957 at 2:00 p.m. in the

Central Baptist Church in Maysville, Kentucky. Charles Newlen, my brother–in–law, served as my best man and Daisy Lancaster served as Oleta's maid of honor. The reception was held at The Avalon, a fine restaurant on the corner of Forest Avenue and Wood Street. It was a gala affair hosted by my parents and Oleta's mother.

My bride and I began our wedding trip. We drove from Maysville through Cincinnati, Ohio, to Indianapolis, Indiana. On Sunday morning we worshipped at the Indianapolis First Baptist Church on the corner of Meridian and Vermont Streets.

That afternoon we traveled north to Winona Lake, Indiana, home of Grace College and Grace Theological Seminary. Winona Lake was the home of Billy Sunday, evangelist and professional baseball player, from 1911 until his death in 1935. Renown musician and evangelist Homer Rodeheaver lived at Winona Lake from 1912 until his death in 1955.

While there we attended sessions of the 14th Annual Convention of the Oriental Missionary Society, which gave us new perspectives on the work God had called us to do. The convention lasted an entire week, June 24–30. However, we had time to attend sessions only on Monday and Tuesday, but we enjoyed them very much.

Tuesday evening, as we headed home, we decided to visit my parents and other family in the Mount Eden area. First we stopped at the home of my grandmother, Lydia Casey. She was so happy to meet Oleta. As we departed, she pressed our hands

Chapter 14 — The Wedding

together, looked at us and said, "You two are the answer to our prayers."

We visited my parents on the farm where they lived. As we left Mount Eden, we had to turn off the main road onto a private road. It was a good mile off the main road to their house. We had to curve our way around a hill until we got to the top. We passed several acres of Burley tobacco, the king crop of Shelby County, and the road headed straight toward a small pond. To the left of the pond stood the old two–story country house, which had been the homestead of my father's uncle, Frank Casey. It was a beautiful testimony to the care and love my father gave it. It had a green and well cared for yard. On the right side of the pond were a barn and milking parlor.

My mother and father were delighted to see us before we returned to our home in Williamson, West Virginia. They lovingly and tenderly welcomed Oleta into the house as a family member and soon had a country meal prepared for us. On Thursday we left the farm and drove off towards Harrisonville. We passed Back Creek and the old homestead of my grandfather, James Henry Casey. I pointed out the house where my father and I were born.

A few more miles up the road I pointed out the grist mill where my grandfather was killed. Before we left Back Creek we stopped at a little dark–looking house perched on the hillside. It was the house of my mother's mother, my grandmother Maud Frazier. We went around to the back door because that is where we would always find her. There she was with her little bonnet pulled down almost over her eyes washing clothes on a washboard. I introduced Oleta to my grandmother. My grandmother was so glad to see Oleta's sweet little face and said so many kind words to her. We had a very nice visit with her. As we were about to leave my grandmother said, "My preacher boy, be good to her."

As we left I had to tell Oleta the rest of the story. Many years ago, when I was just a little boy, my grandfather Everett Frazier walked off one day and never did return. No one ever knew what happened. This left my grandmother Maude to eke out her living alone. She started washing clothes for the neighbors on her washboard using homemade lye soap. She went out in the woods and carried in dead wood and built a fire under an iron kettle located just outside the house. She heated the water and washed clothes all year round. She charged one dollar for a bushel basket full of dirty clothes. For ironing sheets, pillow cases, shirts and fancy pieces she charged a little extra.

"You see," I said to Oleta as we left, "I am the answer to prayer."

Our next little village was Harrisonville where my father first met my mother. So mile by mile Oleta was introduced to my heritage in this rural area of Kentucky.

We quickly cut through the countryside taking U.S. Route 60 to Frankfort, the capital of Kentucky. We continued on from there to Maysville. We stayed only a couple of days in Maysville to rest. After a good rest and a nice visit in Oleta's

Chapter 14 — The Wedding

hometown, we gathered up our things and began our journey together to our home in Williamson, West Virginia.

Chapter 15
The Phelps Mission Is Born

We arrived in Williamson, West Virginia, on Saturday, June 29, 1957, so we would be there for Sunday services at Aflex Baptist Church. The people at Aflex were anxious to meet my wife. They all welcomed her with open arms. It did not take Oleta very long to work her way into the hearts and lives of those people. She focused mainly on the youth.

She proposed and organized a Woman's Missionary Union (WMU) with the women of the church. The response was so great in Aflex that other churches in the area stood in amazement. The WMU was soon carrying food to the needy and clothes to families in the community that were in need.

We also had work in the Phelps area where we were commissioned to start a brand new mission. I had more survey work to complete so I took Oleta along to give her an introduction to the mission field.

We left Williamson with a packed lunch and plenty of water. We crossed the Tug River at Williamson and drove to Belfrey, Kentucky. I was now familiar with all the little villages and winding roads. It was like a little sight–seeing trip for Oleta. We travelled back into West Virginia and passed through Matewan where soon we crossed the Tug River again back into Kentucky. We passed through Freeburn and Phelps, then we took the right fork of Peter Creek toward Coleman until we came to the place I needed to finish my survey. There were several good prospects found along the hollow. In the years that followed, it proved to be worth all of our hard work.

The next program on our calendar was a week-long Vacation Bible School that I had promised the mission at Phelps. It was to be held at the Phelps Court House building, July 8–12, from 10:00 a.m. to 12:00 noon. (See Colossians 3:23). Signs were posted and announcements sent out over the Matewan radio station WHJC. This VBS was the largest undertaking the Southern Baptist Convention had ever undertaken in this part of Pike County.

The staff consisted of Oleta, myself, Della Reed, Deanna Kennedy and a summer worker, who was sponsored by the Home Mission Board of the Southern Baptist Convention. There were forty-eight students enrolled in VBS with an average attendance of forty-one each day. Many had never been to a Bible School before. We gave away Bibles, New Testaments, and other Christian materials. Each day after the VBS, all the workers, Oleta and I, Della Reed, Deanna Kennedy and the summer workers stopped for our lunch we had packed to eat. It was thirty-five miles to Williamson, West Virginia and that was a good hour drive. We would get back to Aflex about 2:00 p.m. each day.

We were certainly in need of a permanent mission site but no suitable property had been found. Mr. Earl Justice, who ran a grocery store in the upper part of Phelps, was one of the men who was committed to supporting Baptist work in the area. He

Chapter 15 — The Phelps Mission Is Born

pledged to contribute to the cause by agreeing to pay the rent for a building for one month.

In the nearby the village of Jamboree, which is just above the Phelps community, we found an old building on a lot covered in weeds. It had no electricity but it was available. Mr. Justice advised us to rent it for one month. That is what we did. We began by cutting down all the weeds. Some one asked the neighbor behind the building if they would allow us to run an extension cord from their house to our building. The neighbor agreed and we promised to pay for the electricity used. Some of the folks brought chairs from their houses. Someone brought a table for us to use along with plates to take up the collection. Someone else brought a high table that we used as a pulpit.

We had a building and we had the furnishings, so we decided to have revival. It would start on August 5th and run all week long. We asked the WHJC radio station in Matewan to make announcements about our revival. We also posted signs everywhere we could.

As a result of this revival, six people had come together—Earl Justice, Edith Justice, Arnold Schwartz, T. J. Ogle, Madge Hurley, and L. J. Hurley—to be the charter members of the Southern Baptist Church of Phelps. We put an end to the mission at Jamboree and continued on at Phelps.

In God's timing, a dance hall in Phelps suddenly went out of business. It was located at the corner of the north fork of Peter Creek, right in the heart of Phelps. We took this opportunity to talk with the owner of the building and were able to rent it. This was an answer to our prayers. For the first few Sundays the mission held its Sunday worship services at 2:00 p.m. because I was still working as full-time pastor at Aflex Baptist Church. How were Oleta and I going to run a new Southern Baptist Church among those who were not Southern Baptists?

Since Oleta and I could not find housing in Phelps where our ministry would be located, we sought a temporary solution. After much prayer and planning, we came up with an arrangement. We would live in Williamson and continue at Aflex on Sunday nights and Wednesday nights. On Sunday mornings, beginning on September 15, 1957, at Phelps we would have Sunday School at 10:00 a.m. and morning worship at 11:00 a.m. On Fridays at Phelps we would hold a youth meeting at 6:00 p.m. followed by a prayer service at 7:00 p.m.

Guilford and Bonnie Jude did a great job at Aflex in Sunday Ministry and outreach in the Aflex Community. I was able to get some preachers to fill the Aflex pulpit on Sunday mornings. The East Williamson Baptist Church in Williamson, West Virginia, agreed to send Wallace and Wanda Ray over a long period of time to help in the development of the work at Phelps. Many others came for a short period of time and did a wonderful job getting things organized. This was a big ministry for the boy from Back Creek, but by this time he was a well-seasoned soldier of the Cross.

God answered one of our long awaited prayers just before the revival we had planned in the spring of 1958. The house

Chapter 15   The Phelps Mission Is Born

directly behind the mission became vacant. It was owned by the same people who owned our mission building. Wow! It could not be any better. God always knows what is best. Some times it is best just to sit back and wait on the Lord. Be patient. God does not always work fast. He has his own schedule. Remember, in Numbers 20 when Moses struck the rock before he was told to and as a result was not permitted to lead the Israelites into the Promised Land.

On April 11, 1958, Oleta and I moved into our house behind the mission building. It had been about two years since I first looked into her eyes as she was folding those bulletins. She informed me she is now pregnant with our first child on the mission field in the remotest section of Kentucky. She has no other family member to lean upon or to pray with. We were about thirty-five miles from Williamson and there were no major grocery stores, no telephones, and only one doctor to serve the entire area. The nearest hospital was about 35 miles away. However, for us, the boy from Back Creek and the girl from 531 Pelham Street, were happy because in our hearts we felt we were in the will of our Father in Heaven. We knew we were not alone. We remembered what we had heard from our mission leaders at the Home Mission Conference. We recalled at our commitment service walking down the aisle once again and saying to God, "I lay my life on the line for you." Oleta and I talked openly about the Mountain Mission Conference at the Oneida Baptist Institute, Oneida, Kentucky. We had discussed with others at the conference about how our area is much different from so many of the others.

The spring revival at Phelps Baptist Mission was one of the most outstanding evangelistic movements to hit Pike County in recent years. Rev. Joe R. Tackett, of Walton, Kentucky, was the evangelist. For Sunday, April 27, 1958, a goal of seventy–five was set for Sunday School. We had one hundred fifty–three people in Sunday School that day. The revival netted a total of forty–two conversions. Thirty–five of these were baptized into the Phelps Baptist Mission at the East Williamson Baptist Church on Sunday, May 5, 1958, at 2:00 p.m. Rev. Tackett said he never in his life witnessed anything like it. People came out of the hollows even in downpours of rain. Some were hauled in trucks like cattle and some walked a mile to the revival at night. (See Psalm 126:6 and 1 John 5:14–15).

Dr. W. C. Boone, the Executive Secretary Treasurer of the General Association of Baptists in Kentucky, and his wife came to Phelps to see for himself what was going on in the community. He had never been to this outpost mission. Dr. Boone looked at Oleta and me and said, "This is the farthest work we have from the main headquarters." The main headquarters was located at 127 East Broadway, Louisville, Kentucky.

Dr. Boone's wife broke in and said, "You all have reached the last frontier in Kentucky. God bless you." (See 1 Thessalonians 5:24).

By this time we had fifty–one members in the mission. God had really blessed the work in every way. I was invited to be a spokesperson at the Schools of Missions in North Carolina. I told the attendees the Phelps Mission story of how God was really moving in the hearts of the people. As a result we received boxes and boxes of clothes for the needy people in our beloved mountains. (See 1 Thessalonians 5:18).

Chapter 16
A Rock In The Mountains

The First Baptist Church in Springfield, Kentucky, where Reverend James D. Hopkins was pastor, heard about the need of the Phelps Mission for property to build a church. Although they were about three hundred miles away, they wanted to come and look over a sixteen-acre property for sale before purchasing it for the Phelps Baptist Mission. They decided to buy this track of land for five thousand dollars from Dr. C. M. Bentley, who lived in Freeburn and was the only local doctor in that part of Pike County.

A great celebration was set for the first Sunday in August of 1958. In one year since it was started, the Phelps Baptist Mission now had a piece of property of their own, deeded in their own name, and absolutely free. Genesis 18:14 says, "Is anything too hard for the Lord?" and Matthew 17:20 says, "Nothing shall be impossible unto you."

Oleta was expecting our first child at any time. She was devoting much of her time and energy planning the anniversary event. On Saturday, August 2, 1958, the little mission field was buzzing with activity. People were coming and going around our house because that's where the big table for the food would be located. The table was placed in our backyard under the big shade tree. It was a fun filled day around the mission and our house.

By 8:30 p.m. Oleta felt we should leave for the hospital. She was already seeing Dr. Henderson in Williamson, so we knew how long it took to make the drive. The drive to the hospital took about an hour, assuming there was no train on the tracks. If there was a train it would take another ten minutes.

We made it to the Williamson Memorial Hospital in Williamson, West Virginia, without any difficulties. Dr. Henderson suggested I stay occupied during the wait. I called our friends, Mr. and Mrs. Wallace Ray, who lived at 1012 Mitchell Avenue. I waited at their home until I received a call from the hospital.

When I got to the hospital Oleta introduced me to our baby girl. She weighed six pounds and thirteen ounces. She was born August 2, 1958, at 10:43 p.m. I spent some time with Oleta and our new daughter, whom we named Sibyl Lynne. When it was time to leave I kissed them both and left thanking God for this precious event in our lives.

Returning home was such a lonely ride. I kept reassuring myself I was not alone. In fact, I had to get back to the work Almighty God had assigned to Oleta and me. Oleta's words to me kept repeating in my mind, "Jim, get back to the Mission—go on—those from Springfield are expecting you. I'll be alright. Sibyl will be okay." I knew she meant it. She meant it that night I put the ring on her finger. I could tell by the look in her eyes and the tone of her voice. I had taken one last look at her eyes and kissed her goodbye. I was learning that it costs something to say "Yes" to God.

Chapter 16 — A Rock In The Mountains

The next day the anniversary celebration was a big success and the groundbreaking went off as planned. Rev. Harold Wainscott, pastor of the First Baptist Church of Pikeville; Rev. E. P. Howerton, pastor of the East Williamson Baptist Church; Rev. James D. Hopkins, pastor of the First Baptist Church of Springfield, and several laymen from the church were all involved in the groundbreaking exercise which was held on August 3, 1958, at 2:00 p.m.

During the winter months we distributed clothing, food and vitamin pills that had been shipped to us to distribute to needy families. I would often carry boxes and bags of necessities up hollows and across foot bridges to families of six, eight, and ten people who were in dire need.

It was 1959 and springtime always gave us the opportunity to have a revival meeting at the mission building. I came to perceive the people here in the mountains liked hell fire and damnation preaching and plenty of it. They liked it straight from the Old Book. Dr. J. S. Bell, pastor of the First Baptist Church of Hindman, Kentucky, was an admired mountain preacher because he used the Old Book and the mountain people loved him.

On Sunday, July 19, 1959, our second child, James Lyndon, was born at the Williamson Memorial Hospital. Lyndon, as we called our son, was God's gift to Oleta and me as we approached the second anniversary of starting the Baptist mission work at Phelps. We observed the second anniversary of the Phelps Baptist Mission, as well as our daughter Sibyl's first birthday, on Sunday, August 2, 1959. We had food, fellowship, singing, games, and other entertainment.

We were blessed and fortunate to have a lot of guest speakers to assist us at the Phelps Mission. There were Rev. Grant L. Jones of Lewisburg, Tennessee; Rev. John H. Hammatt, song leader and associational missionary of Pike County, Kentucky; Rev. Wendell Belew of the Home Mission Board of the Southern Baptist Convention, Atlanta, Georgia; and Rev. S. Lee Sloat, pastor of the First Baptist Church, Belfry, Kentucky.

Miss Elsie R. Hayes of Memphis, Missouri, came to teach at Phelps High School as an art teacher and to work in the Phelps Baptist Mission as a tentmaker, a self–supporting worker in the mission field. She was sent out by the Southern Baptist Tentmakers Program. Fred A. McCaulley, Director of the Southern Baptist Convention Tentmakers, said she was the first tentmaker ever sent to Kentucky. Elsie stayed in our guest bedroom until she found her own place to live. In a year's time she would be chosen as the Honor Tentmaker of 1960.

Billy J. Bryan and his wife, and Ollie Chessur came into the mountains from Western Kentucky. Billy and Ollie assisted in the mission in any way possible. They became valuable workers with the youth. Billy was also a teacher at the Phelps High School. He was a blessing to the school and to the mission work. Ollie only stayed one year and returned to Louisville. The Bryans stayed two or three years and returned to their former home. Rev. Reginald W. Johnson, a song leader,

Chapter 16 — A Rock In The Mountains

and Rev. W. L. Crumpler, both from Bracken Association in Kentucky, assisted the mission in a most successful and heartwarming one-week revival. Rev. Ben Landrum, pastor of First Baptist Church, Jenkins, Kentucky, was a gifted soul winner. He was on the mission field with me walking up hollows and talking the talk for Christ.

Daisy, Oleta's sister, came to Phelps two summers as a volunteer to help in Vacation Bible School. We would have Vacation Bible Schools in one-room schools that had been closed because of consolidation. There was no electricity and the windows were all boarded up. The only light was what came through the doorway. We had Vacation Bible Schools at places like Smith Fork, Coleman and Beech Creek. Each of these were once a public one-room school house. We carried in all the supplies we would need as well as the food and water. We had no piano or other musical instruments. The work was hard for the boy from Back Creek, but these people needed to hear about God. We all did what we could do. We talked with the folks, played with the children, and told stories about Jesus. Each day we told the children that if they wanted to hear more preaching and singing then they could come back that evening at 6:00 p.m. with their parents. We returned each night. Some nights there were only five or six people, and other nights there were twenty or more. We told them about Jesus, the Phelps Baptist Mission, and our love for them.

At Freeburn we used part of a store. The store owner trusted us to use the building. We had to navigate our way around feed bags and other store items on the floor. We sang and taught from the Bible. It was a good way to get the message out to the owner too. Daisy was good at it. Her tender way always won the hearts of the little children.

Georgetown College, Georgetown, Kentucky, sent mission teams to help out. Cumberland College of Williamsburg, Kentucky and Campbellsville College of Campbellsville, Kentucky also sent mission teams. These teams were very inspiring to the youth. They encouraged them to go to college and to be great Christians no matter what path they took in life. This also gave the college students an opportunity to witness the work and develop their evangelical techniques. We left no stone unturned to develop the people in expanding growth in their personal lives. In turn, we helped the community to see the advantage of working for a common goal. Moreover, we blazed an awareness of the work to be done and taught leaders what had to be learned.

In addition to the WMU, Oleta initiated the Girls in Action (GA's) program within the mission field. The GA's is a missions discipleship organization for girls in grades 1–6. The WMU and GA's were all organized and doing their mission work. Oleta was leading these and the local church ladies were responding well. They had several text teachings and all were interested in foreign missions and spreading the Gospel to the end of the world. I organized the Royal Ambassadors program, which is a Southern Baptist organization for boys in grades 1–6. The goal of the RA's is to teach young boys to be committed

Chapter 16 — A Rock In The Mountains

to being Christ–like. The organization got its name and motto —We are Ambassadors for Christ—from 2 Corinthians 5:20, "Now then we are ambassadors for Christ."

Mission work in the mountains needed a unique approach if we wanted to be able to connect with the mountain folks. These are some approaches I found successful. We put together packages of gospel tracts for households, so there was something for everyone in the family. I employed my Royal Ambassador boys to deliver these packages to the front porches of every house in a targeted area.

The Mount Moriah Baptist Church of Mount Eden, Kentucky, asked my father to deliver a truck load of clothes to our mission. I sometimes carried boxes of used clothing as I drove along the hollows. People were invited to look into my car to find suitable clothing for their family. This allowed time to minister to these people.

At the Phelps Baptist Mission, we had a bus to transport people to and from the services. We were able to expand this way. Some people caught my attention as I drove in the community. I noticed a man sitting on his front porch one day. I got out of my car, made my way up the hill bank, crossed the railroad track and reached his porch. He told me he had one eye. I told him about our Mission and the bus transportation. On the next bus trip he was on the road ready to get on. He got saved in a short time and I baptized him on September 6, 1959. This man was James Biliter and he read the entire Bible by

December. When our new church was completed he became a teacher of the junior boys class.

The bus was an important item in our ministry. If the winter temperature dropped below fifteen degrees, the bus had to be kept warm through Saturday night so it would be ready to pick up folks for Sunday morning service. I had the bus parked near our kitchen door and I would get up several times during the night to start the bus engine. I am reminded of 2 Chronicles 20:17 NIV, "You will not have to fight this battle. Take up your positions; stand firm and see the deliverance the LORD will give you, O Judah and Jerusalem. Do not be afraid; do not be discouraged. Go out to face them tomorrow, and the LORD will be with you."

In the summer we used empty one–room schools at Coleman, Smith Fork, and Beech Creek to hold week–long Vacation Bible Schools. This allowed us to reach a larger number of children. In each school we enrolled twelve to twenty–five students. We carried our supplies with us and remained flexible. Our work in the mountains did not fit a typical mold.

Mr. Earl Justice, who owned the Justice Super Market in Phelps, sponsored me on the Matewan radio station WHJC for 15 minutes, one day each week. I would either go to the station or send in an audio tape. This was a good outreach for people beyond our physical reach. Many of our mountain people liked to be baptized in running water, following the model of Jesus. We used Peter Creek, which was next to the Mission. In the

Chapter 16 — A Rock In The Mountains

youth department we enrolled James Wolford, who was soon saved. James was illiterate and spoke with a stutter, yet one night he asked if he could sing a solo. James got up and sang two stanzas of "Jesus Loves Me."

We had thrust our utmost into the work at Phelps. The mountains had come alive with the gospel.

Chapter 17
The Home Front

Our house was deeply involved in the ministry, adapting as needed. At times the adult men's Sunday School class met in our kitchen, the ladies class met at our dining room table, and the nursery was filled with children, including ours. Many mission visitors and speakers would stay in our guest bedroom.

Rev. G. R. Pendergraph from the General Association of Baptists in Kentucky arrived to map our church field. We worked at the dining room table with the map and his tools until 2:00 a.m. If the disciples of Jesus left all to follow Him, we should be willing to burn the midnight oil for Him.

We were still in the process of establishing our Casey household, so we had to be resourceful. Sometimes we learned the hard way, especially since we were somewhat isolated in the mountains. One day as Oleta cooked, the grease in the hot pan caught fire. I quickly put a cover on the flaming pan and attempted to carry the dangerous pan out the back door. While still in the kitchen, I slowly lifted the lid to see if the fire was out. The contents ignited onto my body, burning my right hand severely. To my dismay, fire ran along the kitchen floor. Oleta nervously administered first aid and drove me to the Williamson Memorial Hospital. I had third degree burns which took the skin from the top of my hands. My thumbnail was about gone. The doctors did a good job and indicated I would heal with time. The boy from Back Creek was knocked down but not out. I did not miss a preaching schedule. Oleta had called the Louisville office telling them what happened and prayers went up for us from all over the state.

We kept a large garden so our family was well supplied for the dinner table. We raised potatoes, tomatoes, onions, corn, beets, carrots, cucumbers, squash, and green beans. The neighborhood women taught Oleta how to can our harvest for later use. In mountain fashion, the canning was done outdoors in a large tub of boiling water. I had to set the tub on bricks to keep it above and out of the fire.

The early years at home were happy but meager. At first, we had neither radio nor television. We didn't have a telephone and we didn't even have a Christmas tree our first Christmas. By the second Christmas, we had a tree but couldn't afford decorations. Oleta hung home–made popcorn strings around the tree. But we had Jesus, the reason for the season, and we also had Sibyl to laugh and play with.

Whatever our lot, we put it all in the hands of the Lord. At times our pockets were almost empty financially, but we knew God is on His Throne. And we came through! Psalm 27:1 says, "The Lord is my light and my salvation; whom shall I fear? the Lord is the strength of my life; of whom shall I be afraid?"

The Phelps Post Office was located in Frank Dotson's store. It was a convenient spot to loaf around a bit and talk about the town news. Of course I visited there regularly to deposit or receive my mail. One day when I went to pick up my mail at mailbox number forty–six, I found an envelope from a

Chapter 17 — The Home Front

woman I did not know. I hesitated to open it and pocketed it until I got home. Later at home I opened the letter and showed it to Oleta. It contained a check for fifty dollars. It was sent by a woman from Worcester, Massachusetts, but neither one of us knew of her. In fact, as far as we knew, even the Mission Board had no contact with her. It must be of God! I referred to 1 Kings 17:1–16 and recalled God's promise to me that day in room 318 of Pawling Hall at Georgetown College, "If you will take care of My business, I will take care of you." I remembered too that when I had put the ring on Oleta's hand in Maysville, she had committed to a life in the dark hollows of Pike County, Kentucky. With tears in our eyes, yet joy in our hearts, we marveled at yet another miracle. The love and provision of God knows no limits. (See Psalm 27:14).

The Home Mission Board wanted to keep us informed and to also share our work with other missionaries. To this end, we traveled to the Ridgecrest Baptist Assembly in North Carolina and the Oneida Baptist Institute in Kentucky every year. The Board paid our expenses and it was a refreshing time for our children as well as ourselves.

In August 1960 Rev. Wendell Belew of the Home Mission Board in Atlanta, Georgia, asked me to attend the Glorieta Baptist Assembly, in Glorieta, New Mexico, to give my testimony and speak about the ministry in Phelps. His office paid our expenses as we drove out West. It was a wonderful trip. We got to see many beautiful sites like: Colorado Springs,

Pikes Peak, the Continental Divide, Indian Territory, and Santa Fe, New Mexico.

One of the great things that come from attending conferences is the meeting and sharing with other missionaries. One such missionary I loved so much was Rev. Roy Owen, who was in charge of the work in several large mission fields in the great northern states. He often described the work to me. He once said to me, "You are the kind of man we need in the Dakota's." After considering it for a while, I finally consented to go by train from Williamson, West Virginia to Williston, North Dakota. It was a long train ride for a boy from Back Creek. I spent some time looking over the vast area. There were only six people in attendance on the Sunday that I preached. I spent some time in prayer and felt strongly not to move to the Dakota's.

One of the demands on a preacher occurs when there is a death. A baby had died at birth and I was summoned to perform the rite which was to be held at 1:00 p.m. in the home where the baby would have lived. When I arrived a small crowd had assembled in the living room where the baby lay. A small fan was turned toward the baby to keep flies away. I spoke a few words to the viewers and since an undertaker was not affordable, I earnestly assumed the role. I asked those in attendance to take one last look at the child. After everyone had an opportunity to view the child one last time, we nailed the lid on the casket and began the procession to the burial spot on the mountainside.

Chapter 17   The Home Front

Along the way we encountered the baby's grandmother who was physically unable to attend the earlier rite. She insisted on seeing the dead child. We obliged by removing the nailed lid to let the grandmother view her departed grandson. When we arrived at the gravesite there were several men there with shovels eager to get their work done. We lowered the casket into the grave, but before the men could begin shoveling dirt on the casket I spoke up and said, "Let's pray." After the prayer I quoted a Bible verse and then the casket was covered and left in peace.

The boy from Back Creek and the girl from 531 Pelham Street, like mountain folks, discovered we had to be creative to survive winter in the mountains. There was a severe snow storm heading our way. It was already very cold and the snow banks were building higher. Oleta and I both felt our house might not make it through the storm if the electricity went out. Even though we had plenty of coal for the furnace it was not going to be of much use to us since the furnace was tied into the electricity. By 2:00 p.m. the electric power went out over the entire area around us. We were concerned about our two small children so Oleta suggested we move to the Mission building. It had two big coal–fired stoves we could use for heat and cooking. While Oleta gathered all the necessities and the children, I dug a path to the Mission and started a fire in one of the coal stoves. We were very warm and pleased in our new temporary home. Fortunately the power was restored the very next day and we returned to more familiar and pleasant surroundings—our home.

Many people who live in Pike County have the last name of Hatfield or McCoy. I suppose it is because it is not far from the birth place of the patriarch of the famous Hatfield clan. His name was William Anderson Hatfield. He was also known as Devil Anse Hatfield and he was born in Logan, West Virginia. The McCoy's are scattered all over the area. I had the joy and wonderful privilege of being in the homes of both Hatfield's and McCoy's. I also had the honor of baptizing members of each family, which happened over the few years that Oleta and I had been in the area.

Chapter 18

A Time To Move On

The land for the Phelps Baptist Mission was graded in the summer of 1960 by Arnold Schwartz. He used his bulldozer moving dirt from the side of the mountain in preparation for the future building. Day after day he worked until he had finally cleared enough level land for a building and for parking a few cars. The construction of the building was started shortly afterwards, but was not completed until after the first of the year. We had to raise the money ourselves to begin this event. (See Matthew 6:34 and Psalm 119:105).

Early in 1961 and shortly after the mural was painted on the baptistry wall, eighty members moved into the sanctuary of the Phelps Baptist Mission, which could hold as many as two hundred fifty people. Rev. J. Edward Cunningham, of the General Association of Baptist in Kentucky, and Rev. James D. Hopkins, of Springfield, spoke at the dedication service.

The owner of the house in which we were living wanted it back so I had to move the family. Wallace Ray owned a house on Widow's Branch and he allowed us to move in there in a short amount of time.

I had seen the Baptist work grow from zero to its present size. Our Sunday School was growing, the Vacation Bible School was a continuing success, and we continued making visitations throughout the area.

One Saturday, Oleta and I took our children, Sibyl and Lyndon, to Beattyville to look over the mission field in Lee County, Kentucky, and to visit the church field in Beattyville. I had heard that they were looking for a pastor, so I had previously arranged to preach at the Beattyville Baptist Church for the Sunday morning service and to meet with the Search Committee.

When we arrived in Beattyville we looked for Aunt May's Motel on Route 11, where we had reservations. Aunt May, a member of the church, greeted us with a warm, welcome smile. It felt good to be among friendly folks and we looked forward to the night's rest. We thanked God for His goodness to us. (See Jeremiah 33:3 and Psalm 32:8).

On Sunday morning I was prepared to give my sermon in the pulpit. I preached and Heaven came down and God kissed the service with His blessed presence. Later I met with the Search Committee and found a oneness in spirit.

I felt we had established the basics here at Phelps. The further development of the Mission could be handled by others. Oleta and I discussed the possibility of this new opportunity at Beattyville and agreed to accept the position if it was offered. It seemed like it was time to make a move. I believe the Lord confirmed this when I was offered the position to pastor at Beattyville Baptist Church. I replied to the committee that I would accept the position and I would be prepared to preach on Sunday, August 6, 1961.

Chapter 18 — A Time To Move On

I resigned from Phelps Baptist Church and conducted my last services there on Sunday, July 30, 1961. The next day we began our move to Beattyville.

In addition to being called as pastor, I had also been called as missionary for all of Lee County. One of the missions was called Lower Creek Baptist Mission and was located within Beattyville. Another mission was called Eager Mission. It was located on Highway 52, going towards Irvine, at Crystal, Kentucky. This mission work was a great blessing to the church and the entire community. It was a challenge that the boy from Back Creek and the girl from 531 Pelham Street accepted.

During our first year in Beattyville, Oleta initiated the Girls in Action and won the hearts and confidence of the girls. They loved their new teacher. The Woman's Mission Union, under the direction of Oleta, met regularly and expanded their mission, reaching the lost and needy in the community.

A pastor shepherds his flock so I was often called upon when a crisis hit one of our families. It was a sad day when Mrs. Anna Lee Tirey, wife of Freddy Joe Tirey, died at her home early Tuesday morning April 3, 1962. She was a young mother and a member of our church. I preached the memorial service and presided at the burial in River View Cemetery. The most difficult burden was to console the grieving family.

By spring of 1962, I was considering a county–wide revival for Baptists. As the plans unfolded, I contacted Rev. Homer Martinez of Fort Worth, Texas, as the evangelist. The newspaper in Beattyville printed the following article to help us get publicity.

> The Baptist Churches of Lee County will have a county-wide revival May 27–June 3, 1962. The Churches and Missions participating in the campaign are Beattyville Baptist Church, Lower Creek Baptist Mission, Eager Mission, Heidelberg Baptist Church, and Stone Coal Baptist Church. Rev. Homer Martinez of Fort Worth, TX is the evangelist. The song leader is Douglas Scott of Greenville, SC. Services will be held each night at 7:30 PM at Beattyville Baptist Church. Rev. James E. Casey, Jr., Pastor.

This revival was the turning point of evangelism in Lee County. Folks from all walks of life responded heartily to the Lord as His message echoed through the hollows for years to come. The Congregation continued in faith as three new deacons were ordained on June 17, 1962—James Eversole, Fred Moore, and Omer Caldwell. To improve the quality of the Vacation Bible School I provided my leadership and guidance. I also enlisted pastors from the surrounding local area, as well as from the Southern Baptist Theological Seminary in Louisville, to preach at the missions.

Beattyville is at the junction of three forks—North Fork, Middle Fork, and South Fork—that form the mighty Kentucky River. This area was flooded twice, causing great damage to businesses and houses, while we lived in Lee County. Our third

Chapter 18 — A Time To Move On

child, Jeffrey Dale, was born on August 24, 1962, at Central Baptist Hospital in Lexington. He weighed in at 7 pounds 8 ounces at 9:55 p.m. He brought a lot of joy to our family and to the congregation.

In time I made good friends with doctors, teachers, business men, and farmers. These folks were very instrumental when we needed help in the community. Many men of God in the county joined in to help in the Missions and Churches. Dr. W. H. Curl, from the General Association of Baptists in Kentucky, and Dr. Harold Sanders, of the State Convention, cooperated to supply their expertise and staff whenever I needed their assistance to get the word of our Lord to the people. We were very blessed to have and use these human resources.

In the spring of 1963 I planned another county–wide Baptist revival. Rev. Winn T. Barr, pastor of the First Baptist Church in London, Kentucky, agreed to be our evangelist. This revival was held April 7–14, 1963, at the Beattyville Baptist Church. The revival participants included Lower Creek Baptist Mission, Faith Baptist Church, Stone Coal Baptist Church, and Heidelberg Baptist Church. This large group working together made a great impact on Christian Ministry in Lee County. It says in 1 Kings 8:56, "There hath not failed one word of all his good promise."

I held a revival at Thomas Baptist Church, a country church in Estill County near Irvine, Kentucky, in August 1963.

Mrs. Lena Lightfoot, a member at the Lower Creek Baptist Mission, asked Oleta to preside over the organization of a Busy Bee Circle for the women in the area. We were having many new experiences as we expanded our printing ministry. I told Oleta the mimeograph machine was a big improvement over the old hectograph duplicator we had at Phelps. With the hectograph duplicator you first had to create a master document using various inks, then transfer the image to a gelatin surface treated with glycerin. Finally copies were made by pressing paper against the gelatin surface. The new mimeograph machine saved a lot of time, was not nearly as messy, and produced a much better product.

Our church was part of the Red River Association of Missionary Baptists in Kentucky and I had the privilege of serving as moderator for this organization for one year. We also sponsored a Schools of Missions Program with guests from all over the world, representing the many nations where our missionaries served. We began a church library which consisted of over a hundred books. Miss. Freddye Cole was elected to serve as the church librarian.

"Ah Lord God! behold, thou hast made the heaven and the earth by thy great power and stretched out arm, and there is nothing too hard for thee" (Jeremiah 32:17).

In order to expand our knowledge and learn new skills, Oleta and I went to the Ridgecrest Baptist Assembly, North Carolina, in August. They held sessions for the children, thus our whole family benefited from this conference. The Mission

Board also sent us to the Oneida Baptist Institute in Oneida, Kentucky. Not only did we experience spiritual enrichment, we had precious time to share God's work with other missionaries. (See Psalm 28:7).

Chapter 19
The Call To Wheelwright

Oleta and I were experiencing a burden for the deep mountains when I heard God's urge to move on. In November 1963 I took the family to Wheelwright, Kentucky. I preached at the First Baptist Church of Wheelwright and interviewed for the position as pastor. Oleta and I certainly enjoyed the ministry at Beattyville but there was something about the challenge at Wheelwright that just drew me out. I had a deep feeling this was God's will for us at this time in our lives.

Wheelwright began as a tent mining camp in 1916, but after Inland Steel Company took over the mining operation, it was a model coal town. The town was very clean, dotted with nicely painted houses and held a population of about eight–thousand including the surrounding villages. The town had a public swimming pool, a clubhouse, a theatre, a laundry and dry cleaners, a telephone company, a doctors office, and a hospital. They even had a 9–hole golf course, and established Methodist and Baptist churches.

Soon thereafter I was extended a call to come to Wheelwright to be their pastor. The decision to move and minister in Wheelwright, Kentucky, was not an easy one for us. We enjoyed Beattyville and yet we continued to feel it was time to make a move. After thought and prayer, I tendered my resignation at Beattyville Baptist Church as of December 29,

1963. I accepted the call to the First Baptist Church of Wheelwright effective January 5, 1964.

As the year ended we headed for our new beginning in our new mission field and new home in Wheelwright, Kentucky. The house was located near the church and close to several shops.

On May 31, 1964, our third son, Stephen Barry, was born at the McDowell Hospital at 4:57 a.m. Barry, as we called him, weighed seven pounds and eight and one–third ounces, and was twenty inches in length. This brought new excitement to the church nursery. Oleta became active in the nursery. The nursery was in need of a good storage cabinet, so one of our church members, Hodley Osborne, built it.

The First Baptist Church of Wheelwright drew people from nearby villages—Melvin, Weeksbury, Burton, McDowell, Drift, Minnie and Price. The church sponsored two missions, Jack's Creek Baptist Mission and Lambert Baptist Mission. Jack's Creek was about five or six miles from the Wheelwright church. The Lambert Baptist Mission was located near Hi Hat.

I had to juggle my schedule between Jack's Creek and Wheelwright as I conducted the services at each site. Brother Hodley Osborne was a great help to me. He was the mission leader at Jack's Creek so he would open up the building and get things ready. I would preach at Jack's Creek mission first and then I would drive back to Wheelwright and preach there. This did not matter to the boy from Back Creek as long as souls were being won to Christ.

Chapter 19: The Call To Wheelwright

Harve Johnson was the pastor of Lambert Baptist Mission. It was a well organized mission and they soon asked the Wheelwright church to let it be a fully organized Baptist church. On June 20, 1964, I called a council together and Dr. Harold Sanders, executive secretary of the Kentucky Baptist Convention, brought the constitutional message. As a result, the Lambert Baptist Mission received its status as a Baptist church and became the First Baptist Church of Lambert.

On one very cold Sunday morning—the temperature had dropped to about ten degrees Fahrenheit over night—Brother Osborne and I went to the Jack's Creek mission to get all the natural gas heaters lit so the building would be warm for the people. One of the heaters suddenly exploded and as I jumped back I scraped my hand on the heater. As blood gushed from my injured hand, Brother Osborne wrapped a towel around my hand. I stayed and preached the morning sermon. Immediately after the service I drove myself to Dr. Patterson's office where I was given a tetanus shot and treatment for my hand. I continued with my regular church services and preached as usual.

That incident must have given Dr. Patterson a new perception of me, because not long afterwards he knocked on my front door and told me about a coal mine accident. He told me that one of the miners had been killed and asked if I would accompany him to tell the miner's wife the unpleasant news. A shepherd must tend his sheep. I looked back at Oleta who knowingly assured me, "It's alright—it's God's work—go on."

As we approached the home where the miner had lived, the miner's wife was already anxiously peering from the window. The presence of a doctor and a preacher was unmistakable. She met us as we reached the porch and cried out, "My God, oh my God." The doctor confirmed her fears. She now knew that her husband was the one who had been killed.

After that experience, Dr. Patterson and I became life–long friends. As I returned home and related the sad episode to Oleta, she explained, "God put you there this morning for that purpose, so you could minister in time of need."

A similar incident occurred not too much later. The victim could have retired earlier but felt the coal mine work was all he knew. On that fateful night he was killed while driving a mine vehicle. The miner's co–workers could not explain the accident. It was 1:00 a.m. and I was trying to find some words of comfort for the grief–stricken widow. She was a member of the Wheelwright church and she loved the Lord. As darkness turned to dawn I left the group of sorrowed family and neighbors and returned home. The boy from Back Creek never dreamed the ministry would demand this when he left the plow handle for the pulpit.

Life was difficult in a coal mining town. One day I heard a loud explosion from the Branham Hollow area. People were aimlessly shouting and screaming in desperate voices. A house had blown up because of a natural gas explosion and a young baby was killed. Why was living so dangerous?

Chapter 19 — The Call To Wheelwright

One day I decided to see for myself what it was like to be in a real coal mine. I asked to visit one of the mines. I had to sign a release freeing the mine of any responsibility. I donned the proper gear and entered the mine via a mine car. We rode in about five miles underground—it was dark, wet and scary. I will never forget that awful experience. It changed by life forever.

As pastor at Wheelwright, I spoke in several Schools of Missions in North Carolina. These presentations stirred up interest in our work in Eastern Kentucky. I attended several other similar week-long conferences. One was in Mobile, Alabama. I spoke at a different church every night. Oleta took me over to Williamson, West Virginia, and I caught a passenger train all the way to Mobile. On the way back home there was some delay, so when I got to Cincinnati, Ohio, I called Oleta. I told her of the delay so she would not worry and would be able to pick me up on time.

Another time I went to Guymon, Oklahoma, by way of passenger train. I remember it was winter and I stayed in a different home each night. There was no train available after the services on Friday evening that would allow me to get back in time for Sunday morning services. I cancelled my train ticket and bought an airplane ticket. I flew from Wichita, Kansas—to Topeka, Kansas—to Kansas City, Kansas—to St. Louis, Missouri—to Louisville, Kentucky—and finally to Lexington, Kentucky. I had called Oleta and asked her to meet me at the airport. When I got off the airplane it was a real homecoming. There was Oleta, all my children, and my mom and dad all waving and cheering. The boy from Back Creek was back home in Kentucky. We had a great reunion in the airport, hugging and kissing one another. It was great to be in God's service and know your family was behind you.

I also attended several Schools of Missions in Kentucky. One time I went to Fulton in western Kentucky with Rev. Ray Cummins, pastor of the Campton Baptist Church. I drove to Campton and left my car there. We drove the rest of the way to Fulton in his car. It was a good experience but I sure was glad to get back home.

The Home Mission Board and the State Mission Board continued to send Oleta, my family, and me to Ridgecrest Baptist Assembly in North Carolina and to Oneida Baptist Institute in Kentucky. These provided us great opportunity to grow in our ministry and teach others what we had learned.

Every year the Baptists gathered in Louisville for an Evangelistic Conference held at the Walnut Street Baptist Church. Guest preachers throughout Kentucky come with burning hearts and a zeal for lost souls. They challenged the audience to win souls in their communities. Dr. R. G. Lee and Dr. W. A. Criswell had a way of bringing the congregation to tears, lamenting over lost souls.

Back in Wheelwright, I was using many resources to reach the unsaved. I had a 16mm movie projector and I used it at various places in the community to show movies provided by the Billy Graham organization. I also showed various mission

Chapter 19 — The Call To Wheelwright

slide pictures. I tried to be visible and active at school activities. Mr. Boone Hall, principle of Wheelwright High School, was a member of our church and frequently asked me to participate at graduations, basketball and football games, and other school activities. I was never ashamed to ask people to help us reach boys and girls in the community. I was able to get a few people from a church in Louisville to help us out at Jack's Creek Baptist Mission for Vacation Bible School.

I once told a store owner how great it would be to have an ice cream party on the last day of Vacation Bible School. He agreed and on the last day he brought plenty of free ice cream. People in the mountain hollows liked to see leaders stepping out in faith for their children. Free ice cream on a hot night! The Bible says that if you ask, you will receive. The Beaver Creek Kiwanis Club elected me as an honorary member. The members met weekly and did many good things for the community. I also served on the Wheelwright City Council.

Wheelwright is a the southern tip of Floyd County and only about twelve miles from the Virginia state line. Its two–thousand people were nestled in three–hundred eighty-four houses between the hollows. It was the last company–owned coal town in Kentucky. The town began when Elk Horn Coal Corporation began coal development in that area. In 1930 the Inland Steel purchased the mine and the town prospered. Island Creek Coal Company purchased the mine and the town in 1965 and then a year later sold it to Mountain Investment, Inc. for 1.3 million dollars. In this deal, Mountain Investment received all the houses, business properties, and utilities. There was now no local ownership of the water, gas, electric, sewage disposal, television and telephone systems. Moreover, the clubhouse, swimming pool and library, which were once the hallmark of this ideal mining town, went the same route.

A rumor spread that Inland Steel was opening a mine in the Mount Vernon, Illinois, area. Many of the unemployed miners abandoned Wheelwright and hastened with their families to Mount Vernon. Before our eyes our hometown was becoming a ghost town. Depression blanketed the community as even our church attendance rapidly dwindled. Our ministry was highly affected as we had just called a pastor at Jack's Creek Mission, which was also swept under.

I consulted Dr. A. B. Colvin of the Kentucky Baptist Convention about the dire situation. He remarked that perhaps I should ask God about getting out rather than trying to stay.

It wasn't long until I learned that the First Baptist Church of West Liberty, Kentucky, was seeking a pastor. Oleta and I, and all the children, drove to West Liberty in pursuit of this new mission site. I preached, interviewed, and looked over the mission field in Morgan County. The First Baptist Church of West Liberty extended me a call to be their pastor. I accepted.

I resigned from the First Baptist Church of Wheelwright effective June 30, 1968. During my pastorate there we added sixty-six new members to the church. I hated to leave but it seemed the correct thing to do as a young pastor.

Chapter 20

On To West Liberty

The First Baptist Church of West Liberty, Kentucky, sent a truck to Wheelwright to move our belongings to the church parsonage at 111 Peddler Street. I was to assume my duties as pastor and Morgan County missionary on July 1, 1968. The boy from Back Creek and the girl from 531 Pelham Street were on the way to another new beginning.

The church had not conducted its Vacation Bible School as yet so Oleta and our children used this opportunity as a good way to get acquainted with the church people and the children in the community.

The preceding pastor, Rev. Edgar Tandy, had succumbed to a sudden heart failure in the midst of the Church Building Program. The church members were in disarray having lost excellent leadership. However, the work of the Lord had to continue. My primary concern as pastor was to be a shepherd of the flock. The members were scattered throughout Morgan County, so I had to locate their whereabouts. Lost and unchurched people needed a fresh visit from a man of God. The youth in the community needed someone to rally around lest they fall away. The children must not be overlooked in our busy and hurried lifestyle or they will drop out of church life.

First I met with the deacons and other church leaders to see where we were in regard to the new building. We studied our financial situation and determined to complete the construction. Some of our men were willing to donate time and labor which would save money and get the job finished quicker. With these factors in place, we agreed to complete the new church building.

To get my bearings, I attended the Red River Association of Missionary Baptists in Kentucky. Both the State and Foreign Mission Boards gave wonderful reports and there was a good spirit of cooperation and participation among the churches. We joined the local Ministerial Association, which combined efforts with other city churches in West Liberty, to plan Thanksgiving and Easter services. These were a blessing to the community and helped the folks see the value and concern of the community churches. Since we had two children in the public school system, Oleta and I got involved in the local Parent–Teacher Association. This helped us build relationships in the community.

I had long wanted to be part of the Billy Graham Crusade. I was invited to be part of the Pittsburg Crusade, which was scheduled from August 30 to September 8, 1968. I left right after the Sunday night service on September 1, 1968, and drove all night until I got to Pittsburg, Pennsylvania. I made it for the first session held Monday morning at the Presbyterian Church, which is not far from Pitt Stadium. I attended classes in the daytime and each night I would go to Pitt Stadium for the Billy Graham Crusade. This was work away from home. The boy from Back Creek never dreamed it would be like this.

Chapter 20

On To West Liberty

I recalled at Georgetown College I had signed a paper saying I wanted to be a Baptist Evangelist. Sitting at the crusade among those distinguished men of the cloth, I felt right at home, because I was winning people to Jesus in my little church and on my little church field. My mind's eye went back to that night in front of 531 Pelham Street when I put that ring on Oleta's finger and she accepted my marriage proposal. I knew at that moment she was in prayer for the boy from Back Creek. I could not do what I was doing without her. She was my support, my compliment. I knew she was waiting, praying, and running the household so I could be working at the ministry. As soon as the sessions were over at the crusade, I was eager to get home to return to my helpmate. God got me home safe and sound and she was right there, waiting, arms and heart open for the boy from Back Creek.

The weekend of October 26–27, 1968, was officially set for the dedication of the new church building of the First Baptist Church of West Liberty. On Saturday night, October 26, 1968, Rev. Jesse Bourne, a former pastor now presiding at Smithsboro, Kentucky, preached at 7:00 p.m. Special music was provided by Robin Lee Little, of Melvin, Kentucky.

The next morning, Sunday, October 27, 1968, at 11:00 a.m. Rev. A. O. Allison, of Ashland, Kentucky, gave a prayer for the dedication of the new church building. This was followed by the morning worship service, which was held by Dr. C. R. Daley, of Middletown, Kentucky. A covered dish dinner followed the morning service. At 2:00 p.m. Rev. A. B. Colvin, of Middletown, Kentucky, gave a special report, which was followed by a message given by Rev. Gordan Duncan, of Ashland, Kentucky. The Sunday evening service was held at 6:00 p.m. and Rev. Bruce Hullette, of Four Mile, Kentucky, gave the closing message.

The cost of the entire building including furnishings was sixty-thousand dollars. The building could house two-hundred people in Sunday School and the sanctuary could accommodate two-hundred and fifty people. This was a great event for the First Baptist Church of West Liberty and the people of Morgan County.

A revival was planned for October 28 to November 3, 1968, with the youth in charge of services and I would bring the message each night. In November, after a traditional Thanksgiving feast, we had ball games for the young ones while the older folks talked about yesterday's world.

When my mother and father came to visit for Thanksgiving, they brought our three boys a young dog. It was one of the pups of my father's dog, Sugar, a beautiful black and white Border Collie. The boys named their dog Rover. Since we did not have a fence, Rover would always wonder over into the yards of the neighbors, causing trouble at times. At Christmas time I took the children along to cut a tree. I had my own system to keep it fresh and green, but it did not work. Oleta decided that would be the last Christmas we would have a live tree. From then on we had an artificial tree.

Chapter 20 — On To West Liberty

The winter months usually brought lots of snow, which slowed things down a bit. I decided that during this slow time I would take a religious survey. I contacted my old friend, Rev. G. R. Pendergraph, who had done this with me before. I did most of the house–to–house visitation while he mapped the mission field and totaled the survey results. He did a remarkable job and I was grateful that he worked along with me on this project. When the survey was completed, the results showed we had several areas the church should address.

Oleta was continuing to lead the GA's and was active with helping the WMU to be mindful of overseas missions. She was a bold pillar. She taught extensively and fearlessly declared the Plan of Salvation with love in her heart and a zeal for God. She had the Biblical formula for victory.

A small radio station in West Liberty broadcast our Sunday night services live from our church sanctuary. This was a great opportunity to reach our shut–ins. Many people responded to our appeals for souls via radio.

In the summer of 1969 we continued our annual trips to Ridgecrest Baptist Assembly and to Oneida Baptist Institute. They were always stimulating. Oleta and the children always looked forward to those events as times of good fellowship, fun, and relaxation.

I spoke at some of the grade schools in Morgan County on a regular basis. Cannel City was one of the places I enjoyed especially since some of my church members lived in the small village of Cannel City.

Time moved on and another Thanksgiving was soon to arrive with all its history and times of remembrances. We thanked God for the pilgrims and our fathers who braved the waters and came to this country. We praised God for our little family of four children and all He had given to us. We thanked Him for our friends, neighbors, a good church, a free country, and a land where we could worship in peace, love, and harmony.

For several years, my friends in Indiana suggested I preach in the Hoosier state. They assured me it was a great place to live and minister. Oleta and I had given it some thought but it did not seem to be right for us at that time. However, we were open to God's leadership.

One day it happened, like a bolt of lightning, I got a call from a church across the Ohio River from Louisville. Oleta and I decided to visit Pleasant Ridge Baptist Church of Charlestown, Indiana, for an interview. We took the whole family to Charlestown. Oleta and the children found the environment favorable. The church was in a building program and since I had experience in this area, I felt this was my calling. I did my best to present the message of God's Word as found in the Holy Scriptures to the Hoosier congregation. I thought, if God wanted us here then it must be a one–hundred percent vote from the church. Otherwise I would let the opportunity pass by.

Pleasant Ridge Baptist Church offered me the position to become their pastor. It was a big decision and a big

Chapter 20 — On To West Liberty

opportunity, but I accepted the challenge. We returned to our home in West Liberty and the next Sunday after preaching my message I read my resignation as pastor of the First Baptist Church of West Liberty effective December 31, 1969. (See John 10:27).

Chapter 21
Reaching Across The State Line

It was a cold winter day when the movers from Charlestown, Indiana, arrived in West Liberty to load our furniture. The boy from Back Creek and the girl from 531 Pelham Street, and their four children were ready for the move across the Ohio River. The men who came to help us move were strong and healthy, but the cold wind made the work hard. Oleta and I packed our two cars and we were ready to bid West Liberty *good–bye*. We were moving to our first home in Indiana.

Pleasant Ridge Baptist Church in Charlestown, Indiana, had a nice parsonage located at 330 Hampton Court in a subdivision called *the Project*. The houses in *the Project* were constructed in the 1940's for civilian workers who built the Charlestown Powder Plant and eventually housed the plant workers. The plant made black powder and other explosives from World War II through Vietnam. After World War II the houses were made available to the general public.

It wasn't very long after we moved in that a church family invited us to a Friday night prayer meeting in their house. Oleta and I were greatly impressed with the deep spiritual movement of God in the hearts of so many of the people here at Pleasant Ridge Baptist Church. Members talked freely and enthusiastically about Jesus, the Bible, God's Holy Spirit, and the need to get out and get souls saved.

One of the first men I met when I got to church that first Sunday as pastor was Fillmore Johnson. He was so fired up that he and I wound up back in the Sunday School class room kneeling in prayer. He carried a burden for lost souls and would go out even in the darkness of night to visit people. My goal was to take bulletins, tracts, and pamphlets to every house in *the Project*. I teamed up with some of the men in the church and we visited people they knew and this helped spread the word of God.

In a business meeting the Church had set aside the dates of April 20–26, 1970 as revival time at Pleasant Ridge Baptist Church with Rev. S. Lee Sloat, from Graham, Kentucky, as Evangelist and Mr. Wilburn Hester as Song Leader.

Oleta, my loyal helpmate, thrust into action. Her class room was a model for others to see. The children loved her and responded to her leadership. Rev. Lew Reynolds, of the Sunday School Department of the Indiana State Baptist Convention, used Oleta as a specialist. He utilized her as a teacher in several Sunday School conferences across the state of Indiana.

Our Vacation Bible School at Pleasant Ridge Baptist Church was one of the shinning examples of what can be done when people work together. Mr. J. C. Richardson was the bus driver and he gave himself to the task completely. He loved the children and this was his place in Kingdom Ministry. Oleta was good at planning extra activities for the children, like a trip to the Louisville Zoo or to Louisville, Kentucky, to interview a Jewish Rabbi.

Chapter 21 — Reaching Across The State Line

J. C. Richardson and Oleta would get together and make plans to go places even after the VBS was over. Popular spots were a trip to Squire Boone Caverns and Village at Mauckport, Indiana, and to Marengo Cave at Marengo, Indiana. The girl from 531 Pelham Street never gave up. She kept pressing on.

In the midst of all that was going on in our church life, our next to youngest son, Jeffrey, had been retained in the first grade by his first grade teacher. It was evident Jeffrey had difficulty with reading and writing. It was discovered that he had dyslexia, which is a language learning disorder in which a person has difficulty reading. Oleta rose to the occasion and found help for those who had this problem in New Albany, Indiana. Oleta quickly called the Southern Association for Dyslexia, Inc. and got Jeffrey enrolled in the New Albany program. Oleta would make sure Jeffrey was there for the classes as they were scheduled after school hours. This program was initiated for Jeffrey and he continued there for several years.

As Oleta and I began to assess our mission field and our roles in it, we assured each other that God had specifically placed us here in Charlestown. Yes, the boy from Back Creek believes Romans 8:28, "And we know that all things work together for good to them that love God, to them who are the called according to his purpose."

Meanwhile, Oleta went quietly about working with Jeffrey, driving him back and forth to New Albany for his schooling and instruction. All four of our children had been bothered by sore throat and coughing. We took them to the local doctor who suggested that all four of them have their tonsils taken out. The date was set and we marched all four of them—Sibyl, Lyndon, Jeffrey, and Barry—to the Clark Memorial Hospital in Jeffersonville, Indiana on August 13, 1970 to have their tonsils removed. All went well with each one.

The Pleasant Ridge Baptist Church had a large number of youth attending all the church services at that time and it was decided that the church should invite a team of students from Cumberland College, Williamsburg, Kentucky, on September 18–20, 1970, to inspire and promote the talents of the youth in the community. A second team of Students came from Georgetown College, Georgetown, Kentucky, on November 6–8, 1970, with the idea of turning the hearts of youth in our area toward Jesus Christ and surrendering to His call for their life's work.

Some of the men in the church were working with the local Boy Scout troop and several boys from the church were also attending the meetings. It was voted on and passed that the Pleasant Ridge Baptist Church sponsor a Boy Scout troop. Our son, Lyndon, joined the Boy Scouts at this time.

The Church ended the year with Mrs. Yvonne Bowling directing a Christmas program entitled *Arise, Thy Light is Come*. God had been good to this church and to Him all praise goes. A total of fifty-four new people had been added to the Church membership in 1970. The average attendance for Sunday School was one hundred fifty-nine. The Vacation Bible

Chapter 21 — Reaching Across The State Line

School had three hundred twenty-three enrolled, which included a Mission VBS.

I had been cautioned that when I crossed the Ohio River I would encounter a different kind of Baptist people. I worked with different kinds of Baptists in Eastern Kentucky. The boy from Back Creek was a Southern Baptist preacher and the girl from 531 Pelham Street also had a history of Southern Baptists roots. However, the Bible was the Word for all of us and we bonded with the Baptists across the Ohio River in spiritual unity.

We promoted the Cooperative Program, the Lottie Moon Christmas Offering, and the Annie Armstrong Easter offering for Home Missions. I wanted this church to have a heart for Missions. We needed to have a zeal for the unsaved in our neighborhood but it should not end there. God's word tells us in Matthew 28:19–20 and in Acts 1:8 that we are to evangelize beyond our borders.

It was January 1971 and I had made about one hundred pamphlets that explained the Plan of Salvation. I wanted them delivered to the houses in *the Project*, but this winter it was a very cold. So I called Charles Thompson to help me. Charles was a member of the church and worked at the Ford Plant in Louisville, Kentucky, but he was not working that day. I informed him it was one degree above zero and we should wrap–up well and walk fast. The plan was that unless someone opened the door we were not going inside. We would just lay this package of material on their door step and continue on. It did not take long and it really was fun doing it in one degree above zero. That's not the end of the story. Later on that year, I guess it was July or August, at the Sunday morning invitation an elderly lady came down the aisle. She had a twisted–up piece of paper in her hand and she said, "Here it is…I found it…I accepted Jesus." It was worth it that one degree above zero day.

My long time and good friend, Rev. Homer Martinez from Fort Worth, Texas, spoke at Pleasant Ridge Baptist Church on January 29–31, 1971. That Mexican preacher really did shake–up Charlestown. Several teen agers were soundly converted and I baptized them into the membership of the Pleasant Ridge Baptist Church.

On March 3–7, 1971 we had four guest laymen as speakers from North Carolina in a layman–led revival. The men paid their own way to Charlestown and they stayed with church members. They visited and witnessed during the day and conducted services each night.

One of my good friends, Mr. Fillmore Johnson, was ordained as a Baptist deacon on March 13, 1971. Fillmore Johnson had a heart for lost souls and spent a great deal of his spare time in visitation. Fillmore was a good carpenter and he did a lot of projects around the church building. He and his wife displayed wonderful talents in God's name. Oleta fell in love with the Johnson family and I remember she once said, "The Johnson's are one of God's trophies."

Chapter 21　　　　　Reaching Across The State Line

The Sunday School classrooms in the basement were now all completed. Oh! They were wonderful. They were large and well decorated with well trained teachers. Nothing could keep these classes from growing. The children were out there in the community. Fortunately we had a church bus to help bring them to the church. We knew that with prayer, hard work, and good teaching we would deliver good results for God.

The Pleasant Ridge Baptist Church voted to invite Rev. Ralph White, of Louisville, Kentucky, to preach the dedication service, which was to be held on Sunday, March 21, 1971. The church was filled with people that day and it seemed that God poured out His Spirit on the congregation in a powerful way. The Charlestown Ministerial Association conducted a crusade at the Charlestown High School March 28 to April 4, 1971. The response in the community was good. The revival seemed to bring the churches from all over the community closer together.

After much prayer, Dr. J. S. Bell, pastor of the First Baptist Church at Hindman, Kentucky, was called as Evangelist for a revival April 25 to May 2, 1971. Dr. Bell was a mission minded pastor, a good soul winner, and a respected citizen of Knott County, Kentucky.

Vacation Bible School at Charlestown made a great impact upon the Pleasant Ridge Baptist Church. J. C. Richardson put his life into driving the bus everyday. He challenged the students by offering to sing a solo if the VBS attendance exceeded its enrollment. That really stirred up the children.

They went home and they asked every boy and girl they could find to come to Vacation Bible School at Pleasant Ridge Baptist Church. Finally it was reported we had broken the record and J. C. came forward and sang "Amazing Grace." It was the Grace of God that had changed J. C. Richardson's life. On May 23, 1971 the youth presented a musical program called *Tell It Like It Is*. The church members were greatly impressed at the talent that was exhibited in the youth department. Great praise went up following the program adulating the devotion of the youth.

God's wonder was magnified many times in the church ministry. The boy from Back Creek and the girl from 531 Pelham Street felt they had made the right decision when they came across the Kentucky state line into Indiana.

Several times I was awakened in the middle of the night by a phone call pleading that I come to the hospital in Jeffersonville, Indiana. Someone was in serious need and begged the boy from Back Creek, now a man of God, to plead their case with the Father in Heaven. Yes, this was part of the calling. Oleta and I did not come to Indiana thinking the work there was either safe or easy but because God had called us. We did not enter upon our present positions with a guarantee of human protection, but rather on the reliance of God's promises.

The annual Homecoming program was set for August 29, 1971. I was scheduled to bring the morning message and Mr. Wilburn Hester was in charge of the song services. The Church hosted the noon meal and the basement dining room was

Chapter 21 — Reaching Across The State Line

decorated in a gracious manner. After the fellowship time, the people gathered back in the auditorium for a gospel singing. Mr. Wilburn Hester was the host and he introduced each one in a gracious way, then he closed the service.

Many of the Church members had a burden for the unreached in the Charlestown community. To encourage them and train them firsthand I accepted an offer from Dr. Jack Stanton of the Home Mission Board in Atlanta, Georgia. He was offering a week's study on witnessing and soul winning in Chicago. I took Dr. Stanton up on the offer and attended his seminar. After the training, I was now prepared and anxious to lead our members to a higher level of maturity. I held a week-long school of witnessing at Pleasant Ridge Baptist Church from September 27 to October 3, 1971. Following this witnessing workshop, the church members were to put in practice what they had been taught. They were to use Psalm 126:6 as their scripture, confident if they sowed God's Word they would eventually reap a harvest. On November 3, 1971, the Pleasant Ridge Baptist Church called Mr. Edward Steigel as Minister of Youth. He was a student at Southern Baptist Theological Seminary, Louisville, Kentucky.

One Saturday night a teen age girl in Charlestown did not reach home from the party she had attended. I had been in the home several times urging the family to be more active in the work of our Lord. However, this young girl decided to go in the wrong direction. That Saturday night, on the way back to Charlestown, she lost control of the car and when it wrecked it caught fire. She was burned to death beneath the wreckage. This was a warning God issued to people in our community, "Be sure your sin will find you out" (Numbers 32:23).

Our Sunday School attendance for 1971 averaged one hundred eighty–seven. Our Vacation Bible School enrollment was two hundred sixty–eight. There was a total of sixty–eight new people added to the church membership. The Pleasant Ridge Baptist Church led an evangelistic conference January 28–30, 1972. One of the following preachers would speak each night: Rev. B. T. Scrivener, pastor of the First Baptist Church, Sellersburg, Indiana; Rev. Elvis Marcum, pastor of the Graceland Baptist Church, New Albany, Indiana; or Rev. Presley Morris, Area Missionary in this part of Indiana and worked with the churches in the Association. The church had a layman's revival February 11–18, 1972, with Rev. Elvis Marcum as evangelist, and Mr. Joel Ragains as song leader.

The following month on March 1–5, 1972, a group of men came from sister Baptist churches to visit people in our community and conduct services at night. This greatly blessed the hearts of the church members to see and hear these men of God speak each night. The committee for the ordination of Mr. Russell Edward Steigel to the Gospel Ministry at Crescent Hill Baptist Church, Louisville, Kentucky, met and he was ordained on April 23, 1972. The next week he held a "Youth Serendipity" program at our church.

Our own children continued to flourish as partakers in our ministry. You can always tell when spring arrives because the

Chapter 21　　　　　　　Reaching Across The State Line

Boy Scouts are usually the first to plan an overnight camping trip. Our son, Lyndon, put on his uniform, proudly displaying his Second Class Scout rank. His troop was ready of a weekend fishing and camping trip.

The annual homecoming of the Pleasant Ridge Baptist Church was set for August 27, 1972. Rev. Lew Reynolds of the State Convention of Baptists in Indiana was the guest speaker. Lunch was served in the basement dining hall for everyone to attend. A gospel singing was held at 2:00 p.m. and was under the direction of Wilburn Hester. Special guest performers were The Kentucky Gospel Singers, from Cadiz, Kentucky, and the Katie Sisters, from Hopkinsville, Kentucky.

Activities were held often to stimulate growth, interest, and participation of the believers. A Harvest Revival was conducted Oct 6–13, 1972, at our church with Rev. B. T. Scrivener, pastor of the First Baptist Church, Sellersburg, Indiana, as the evangelist. It was a great time of rededication by many of the church members and the Lord seemed to be pleased with the revival. God had no doubt called the boy from Back Creek to this demanding work here in Indiana. That girl form 531 Pelham Street maintained her dual position as a strong leader and motivator in the Sunday School programs. She always retained her concern for the unreached people and the elderly. In fact she felt more certain than ever that God had placed her in this Mission field.

Early one Monday morning, I was in Jeffersonville at the Clark Memorial Hospital and I was thumbing through the files in the Clergy's office to see who had come in over the weekend that I might visit. Suddenly, in popped a nurse, almost out of breath, saying, "Are you a minister?" I told her I was a minister. She then began to tell the story about a large truck that had overturned on Interstate 65 near Sellersburg. The driver was here in the hospital and she didn't think he would survive. She said she didn't think the man was prepared to die and asked if I could help. Since he was in surgery I didn't think they would let me enter the operating room, but the nurse told me to follow her. So I did. I followed her up the elevator and into places I had never been before.

I stood in the operating room with doctors and nurses, men and women of great skill and training. I knew, as these experts in their field stepped back from the man on the operating table, as I walked up to him that I could not do anything myself. I opened the Bible in my hand and asked, "Will you believe what I tell you this Book says?"

He nodded and whispered, "Yes."

I read Romans 10:9–13. Then I read Rev. 3:20. I said, "Will you right now invite Jesus into your heart to save you?"

He replied, "Yes."

I then had a brief prayer, thanking God for this man's salvation and pleading God to heal his sick and wounded body. Then I took a few steps back. There was a calm in the room for a moment. Then the medical team stepped forward and resumed their tasks. Tears began to flow as I heard the doctors

Chapter 21 — Reaching Across The State Line

say that he appears to be improving. The nurse and I left. Before I returned to Charlestown I checked and learned that the man, our new believer, had survived and was doing well. In fact, within ten days of the accident he was able to go home to his family in Tennessee.

The year 1972 was about over for the boy from Back Creek and the girl from 531 Pelham Street. Neither one of us ever dreamed our Hoosier mission experience would be cradled by such loving people. We had just finished a dinner with the deacons and their wives when we pondered over how well we were received. Our congregation and the community constantly showered us with beautiful gifts. We really didn't feel that we deserved all this. We had come up in poverty and rags. Oleta cleared my thinking by explaining to me that when Jesus called Matthew, the man just got up and followed Jesus. She told me that's what we are doing. I reminded Oleta that there were some who said we would never make it in Indiana. It's hard to endure when some of your best friends shake their heads and doubt your dreams. Oleta asked if I remembered what God told me there in Pawling Hall in 1951. I did remember. I say it about every day. Then I repeated it once more, "If you will take care of My business, I will take care of you." He has never failed us so far and I believe He will carry us through to the end.

The Lord gave a great year, thirty–seven new people were added to the Church membership with an average Sunday School attendance of one hundred ninety–nine. We had a

Sunday School record attendance of two hundred seventy-three. Vacation Bible School enrollment was two hundred thirty-five. All glory to His name!

In January of 1973 the members of the church had a burden for the unreached in the community. There was a longing in the hearts of the deacons for a moving of the Spirit of God in the church in such a way that it would burst out into the town of Charlestown. I had made the statement I would visit anyone, anywhere, anytime, day or night. That was the offer. I meant it and I stuck with it. I remember crawling out of the bed after midnight several times and driving to the hospital, or hurrying to the house of some drunkard, or to some young couple fighting.

One Saturday night, I got a call to go to New Washington, Indiana. I knew the family and I was familiar with the area. When I got there nothing in my ministry had prepared me for what I was about to witness. I knew that unless God came on the scene nothing could be done. A woman met me at the door. She informed me her husband was dying and was screaming that he would be in Hell shortly. When I walked in the bedroom the man was scratching his arms and body until blood was pouring out. He cried out that something was dragging him down and he would be in Hell in a few minutes. This continued for some time as I stood by the bed. Every once in a while he would rake his hand across his arms and chest, and blood would flow like a river.

Chapter 21 — Reaching Across The State Line

I began to read the Bible. I read Psalm 120:1, Psalm 121:1–2, Psalm 55:1, Psalm 51:1–2, Psalm 32:1, and Psalm 23. I got down on my knees and prayed. I got up and he was still moaning and kicking like a mule with colic. I read John 3:16, Ephesians 2:8–9, Romans 10:9–13, Revelation 3:20, and 1 John 1:9. Then God asked me to grab his arm and command this evil spirit to leave him. I promptly grabbed his arm and held it tightly. I said, "Lord don't let this man die like this. Oh God, drive this evil spirit out of him right now." While I was holding the man's arm, he said, "It's leaving me...It's leaving me...It's leaving me..."

Then he said, "It's gone!...It's gone!...It's gone!...It's gone!" He opened his eyes and he was in his right mind. He looked at me and sheepishly begged, "Preacher, please never tell this to anybody." His wife came to the bedside and he promised that they would be at church the next Sunday.

Another layman revival was planned for March 1–4, 1973, with George Haun as the speaker. This was followed by a youth revival March 18–25, 1973, with students from Hardin–Simmons University, in Abilene, Texas, in charge of the services.

Oleta was thrilled the way the new Sunday School classes were developing. She spent time visiting and talking with people. She was developing strong Christians in the community. Vacation Bible School at Pleasant Ridge Baptist Church once again was drawing the attention of people in the community. The church bus was loaded with children eager to attend Vacation Bible School. Oleta and the other teachers were prepared with a curriculum and materials. This included speakers, field trips, parties, games and much more for all who would attend. Some of the classes had a picnic on the last with hot dogs and ice cream.

Sibyl and Lyndon went to band camp during the summer. They spent a week at Camp Crescendo, Lebanon Junction, Kentucky. They were members of the Charlestown High School Marching Band of Pirates in 1973. Sibyl played the clarinet and Lyndon played percussion instruments, but mainly the snare drum. Lyndon lettered as a freshman on the Charlestown High School 1973 football team. Head Coach Roger Caudill said, "that Casey boy is little but he is tough." Because of that, Lyndon earned the nickname "Buzzsaw" by the coach.

I had been trying ever since I arrived at Charlestown to get some of our members to take a trip to Ridgecrest, North Carolina, for training. I was able to finally convince J. C. Richardson and L. B. Christian to take the trip. I also wanted my father and mother to go with us to Ridgecrest. I finalized the plans and our group set out for North Carolina.

J. C. Richardson and L. B. Christian were in one car. My parents rode in the car with us. We had a great time together. Not only did we learn a lot from the conference at Ridgecrest, we learned a lot from one another.

The boy from Back Creek and the girl from 531 Pelham Street always liked to share and tell others about Jesus. As soon

Chapter 21 — Reaching Across The State Line

as we returned to Charlestown we plunged into the Homecoming, which was on August 26, 1973. Rev. George Waddle, of Berea, Kentucky, brought the morning message. Mr. Wilburn Hester planned a delightful afternoon of Gospel singing. We were blessed with singing from The Ambassadors, from Hopkinsville, Kentucky, and The Kings 4, from Charlestown.

During a business meeting in September 1973, Wilburn Hester accepted the position as Youth Director at Pleasant Ridge Baptist Church.

There were forty-eight people added to the church membership that year. The Sunday School average attendance was two hundred twenty-one and the Vacation Bible School enrollment was two hundred forty-nine.

A new year had begun and spiritual programs continued to flourish. On February 7–10, 1974, Rev. George Haun conducted a glorious revival.

On February 24th the church voted for a new air conditioning system for the nursery and the sanctuary. The music committee was considering the purchase of an organ for the church.

The following month, a youth team from Harden–Simmons University in Abilene, Texas, conducted a revival from March 17–24, 1974, for the teens and young adults in the community.

In the church an aura of stability reigned, so we took some time for major improvements. The trustees and the properties committee reviewed the parsonage property and recommended the church build a new parsonage. On March 6, 1974, the church voted to build it. By May, the committee had the house plans in tact and a twenty-year loan secured to support the project.

For several years the Pleasant Ridge Baptist Church had asked the Clark County road department to maintain that part of the road from State Road 403 to Halcyon Street. Finally, the county agreed to take over maintenance of the road. In a addition, that summer the church property was annexed into the City of Charlestown.

Out in our small back yard was a little tool shed, a shade tree or two and a back fence. On the other side of the fence was a field with trees lining the fence. The boys liked to play on the other side of the fence in the trees. Oleta and Sibyl were out somewhere and I was at home with the boys. Without warning, I heard screaming, yelling, crying outside where the boys were playing. I ran out the front door and around to the back to find blood was covering the head of my son Barry. I wrapped a towel around his head to stop the bleeding. I put Barry in the backseat of the car and I had Lyndon keep pressure on Barry's head. I told Jeffrey to stay home and inform Oleta when she got home. I jumped into my car and headed toward the hospital in Jeffersonville, Indiana. I turned on my emergency lights and drove as quickly as I could. When we got there I rushed the boys into the emergency room. The doctors examined Barry and prepared him for stitches in two places. We breathed a sign of relief as we learned he had no major damage. When we arrived home, Oleta greeted us. The excitement subsided as we unfolded our harried experience. Our family thanked God that He brought us through once more. We gave all the credit and glory to Him.

The church was now settled and the winds of change began to move again. My talent developed in strengthening churches, putting them on a strong foundations, and then turning over committed congregations to able leadership. Rev. C. E. Wiley, of the State Convention of Indiana, for a number of years had been asking me to work farther north in Indiana. The mission field there needed direction, motivation, encouragement, and know-how in church development. The task would not be easy, but God had opened many doors in my past experience.

Shortly thereafter a group of layman from a northern area asked me to come to their church to preach at a Sunday service. I told them that I would never leave my church in Charlestown on any Sunday or Wednesday night. However, if they could arrange for a Friday night service, then I would agree to come to their church. They were able to schedule a Friday night service, although it was out of the ordinary to get a Sunday congregation out then.

I drove the one hundred miles alone to that northern Southern Baptist Church. When I got there the parking lot was full of cars. I entered the church sanctuary and it was filled. Even the choir loft was filled. All of this on a special Friday night to hear the boy from Back Creek. I had never seen anything like that in my life. The congregation's singing sounded great and the choir performance was wonderful. I went in to preach like the boy from Back Creek always does. As the service closed, I requested that I be given their formal decision before the crowd dispersed. Meanwhile, I went in the back room and prayed that God's Will be done. A gentleman soon came back to where I was waiting and informed me I had been voted in as their new pastor. They asked me when I could begin. I told them I could commence on September 15, 1974.

I returned home to Charlestown after midnight. My waiting prayer partner knew this was a big decision for us. She was ready to move, but her biggest concern was the children. She was worried how would it affect them. I reasoned, "If it is God's will for us to go north, God will care for the children." The next Sunday I preached as if I was going to live in Charlestown forever. After the final hymn, I read my resignation, which shocked the entire congregation. Some cried, some were just stunned, and most did not quite understand why I was leaving. My resignation was effective September 13, 1974. However, my last Sunday was September 8, 1974.

The following days were busy. We were packing a family household. There were last minute house-calls to make and the shut-in's needed an attentive farewell. I also had some loose ends that needed to be tied-up and some business to settle. In retrospect, I had been in Charlestown as pastor of the Pleasant Ridge Baptist Church four years, eight months and thirteen

Chapter 21 — Reaching Across The State Line

days. There had been two hundred thirty-four added to membership of the church and the church building was now in good condition. My work here was finished. The future looked great for the Pleasant Ridge Baptist Church. As our family drove away, we knew as we took that final look, that our labor had not been in vain in the Lord. The boy from Back Creek, with his family, was headed for north Indiana. The new challenge there would begin tomorrow.

Chapter 22

A New Challenge

The moving crew from the First Southern Baptist Church, 520 Sawmill Road, New Whiteland, Indiana, drove right up to the front door of our house at 330 Hampton Court, Charlestown, Indiana on Friday September 13, 1974 and soon loaded our furniture and household goods on the truck. Oleta and I and the four children had already put what things we wanted in the two automobiles of ours so it wasn't very long until we were ready to head north on I–65 toward our new assignment. This new church congregation had seen neither Oleta nor our children. Neither had my family seen this new church field and its surroundings. So here was the girl from 531 Pelham Street, like Abraham of old, going on faith, like a stranger with three boys and one girl. What was going through their minds? What would this county be like? What would the schools be like?

We passed by miles of flat land. Acres of corn and soy bean plants stood ready to be harvested. Finally we turned off I–65 at a highway marker that said Whiteland. We followed this road until we saw a sign that read New Whiteland. Excitement crescendoed as we turned off on to Sawmill Road and passed the First Southern Baptist Church. In a few minutes we pulled up to 132 Southlane Drive, our new residence in New Whiteland, Indiana.

The movers were fast-paced, but careful, and soon had our furniture in our new house. Suddenly it dawned on me that we did not stop at the Pleasant Ridge Baptist Church to get my books and personal possessions to be used in my new office. A New Whiteland church member offered to hook his trailer to his car and drive back for my forgotten belongings. He left like a bolt of lightning and did what he said he would. My books and personal items were at the church building the next day and I commended him for a job well done.

As we unpacked, everybody in the family was setting up his own room and it looked fairly good by Saturday night.

On Saturday morning we had watched some of the bus ministry workers as they were about their business of visitation and recruiting people to ride a bus to Sunday School on Sunday morning.

We all got up early Sunday morning and were anxious to see our new church building and meet new people. Just taking a quick look around the area as we drove to the church, parked and walked toward the side entrance of the church building made me feel good. The buses were unloading children and the bus barn and garage in the distance was full of activity. It looked like the boy from Back Creek and the girl from 531 Pelham Street had a lot to learn in the days ahead. As the congregation continued to arrive, Sunday School teachers pointed out where the different classes were held. I noticed that all the teachers came prepared for the Bible teaching hour. It

Chapter 22 — A New Challenge

looked like this church was moving in the right direction and reaching many people of all ages.

The music director, Mr. Max Squires, and his family arrived, and extended an enthusiastic hand shake and morning introduction. The Sunday School hour soon passed and the sanctuary was filled with people. The choir did a wonderful job and the special music was fitting for my message. It was a great first service and the people were all very supportive of our family. Sunday night was a tremendous time in the Lord's house. The Lord used this first day to bring us all together in love for God and His Word.

After helping around the house on Monday morning, I made my way to the Church to see what was going on and perhaps unpack some of my books. A visitor dropped by the church on Monday morning and asked how things were going. I replied I was no longer anxious about my new situation and I was confident God would carry out His will, and His will is mine. I told him I was happier right now in the Lord than I have ever been, and I enjoyed more leisure of soul, casting more fully every burden on Him who alone is able to bear all. Despite the pressures, Oleta seemed happier than I had seen her in a long time. The secret was that Jesus was satisfying the deep thirst of her heart and soul. I met my church secretary, Mrs. Jan Bell, who was one of our church members. She did a great job in every way and was always kind and helpful. Her wisdom and understanding of the church field was always a blessing. Her husband, Mike Bell, served as our Bus Director and was a true servant of the Lord. When I arrived on the church field I believe there were thirteen church buses. Some of these were spare buses in case one broke down out in the field and needed assistance. The bus routes included the towns of Franklin, Greenwood, Whiteland and New Whiteland. Each bus had a bus captain who was responsible for visiting families in the area where he picked up children. Together the buses would pick up between two hundred and two hundred–fifty people. This contributed to the four hundred to four hundred–fifty in Sunday School.

We had a children's church which met at the same time as the worship service in the sanctuary. Mr. Max Squires led between twenty and twenty–five in the sanctuary choir. Mr. Dave Johnson, lead the youth choir until he decided to attend college.

First Southern Baptist Church sponsored a day care center and kindergarten program. These were directed by Mrs. Bonnie Wigginton, also a church member. There were ten to twelve workers in this ministry and there were between thirty–five and fifty children in attendance.

There were several men who served as deacons and contributed greatly to the growth and development of the church. These men, Morris Lambe, Al Foley, Joe De Witt, Will Childers and Bob Thacker, I believe were still deacons when I left the church.

This new ministry required a great deal from the pastor. One Wednesday after visiting four different hospitals in the

Chapter 22 — A New Challenge

greater Indianapolis area, I was tired as we went to the Prayer Meeting hour. Following that I had yet to attend a committee meeting. Was this intense workload weakening my spirit? My confidant, Oleta cautioned, we did not come here because this work here was either safe or easy, but because God called us. We didn't enter these positions under a under a guarantee of human protection but relying on the promise of His presence. As I toiled on, I helped Oleta understand that there are seven hundred eight on the membership roll of the church. Some lived in the northwest part of Indianapolis. She agreed that I could not do all this work by myself. The boy from Back Creek was looking for different ways to serve people, and meet the needs of people. This was a huge job to do, but through the power of the Lord Jesus the church would not fail.

As the year 1974 closed, we assessed it had been a fruitful year here at New Whiteland. Mr. Max Squires had done a superb job with the Christmas musical production. God had surrounded me and my family with a host of wonderful people.

As we entered in 1975 Oleta visioned great opportunities ahead of us. She reminded me to pray, obey, sow, and abide in Jesus for it all belongs to Him. A Baptist men's retreat was held at Highland Lakes Baptist Center on January 3–4, 1975. This retreat was a kickoff for evangelism that year.

I came up with the idea to encourage the membership of the First Southern Baptist Church to read God's word every day in 1975. I stressed that we needed to fill our minds with God's Word, so the devil would not have a chance to lead us astray.

Then on the first Sunday of the new year I challenged my congregation to join me in reading God's word. I taught that things would go better for them and their families by making God's Word top priority in their lives. We held a very successful Vacation Bible School. Several boys and girls came on the bus from Franklin. Two or three Mexican children came and we were able to minister to their families as a result.

On October 16–17, 1975 the annual Indiana associational meeting was held at our church. This was a good meeting and the reports indicated there was growth in a majority of the churches in the association. The annual meeting of the State Baptist Convention was held at the Speedway Baptist Church in Indianapolis on November 11–13, 1975. The convention drew a large crowd of people as some of the most outstanding preachers in the Southern Baptist Convention were guest speakers. We observed Thanksgiving with praise for founding fathers of the United States. This was followed by a week of prayer for Foreign Missions and the Lottie Moon Christmas Offering on November 30 through December 7, 1975. The church secretary informed us we now had seven hundred forty-three church members as we closed the year 1975. To God be the glory. Thanks for God's love and mercy upon us as a church and nation.

As the church entered 1976, Mr. Max Squires had moved away and it was recommended that Mr. Richard Abbott assume his position. Some of the bus routes were also discontinued and therefore some buses were sold. The buses were often used to

Chapter 22   A New Challenge

take church groups to the various places in Indianapolis, such as the Children's Museum of Indianapolis, the Indiana World War Memorial, and the Indianapolis Motor Speedway Hall of Fame Museum at Speedway. They were used also for longer trips like Kings Island, an amusement park northeast of Cincinnati, Ohio. On one Saturday I remember a bus load of people who were full of excitement and stayed until the final fireworks. We did not get home until about 2:00 a.m. yet I was up and preached on Sunday morning as usual. That was a good way for Oleta and I to relate to a busload of mostly youngsters. I had fun with the youth at New Whiteland and especially playing games with them at Vacation Bible School.

My heart was burdened with the responsibility for the unreached in our area of Indiana, those who never attended any church anywhere, and those who seldom hear a Gospel message of any kind. Being in the Johnson County Ministerial Association gave me the opportunity to preach over the radio station in Franklin, Indiana, one week every two or three months. This was a great way to extend the ministry of the local church, but it was not all the Lord wanted our church to do.

My work load was increasing as I carried on hospital visitations, home gatherings to teach the Word, and house to house contacts. One snowy day I was returning from a visit to a hospital in Franklin when the car suddenly hit a slick place on the road. I landed into a telephone pole. I was spared bodily injury, but the Plymouth Duster was badly damaged.

It was about this time that Oleta was called upon to assume the Director of Kindergarten and Day Care Center in First Southern Baptist Church, because of the resignation of Mrs. Bonnie Wigginton. Oleta, my faithful co–worker, was now fully submitted to the will of the Father in Heaven. I was not worried about her being able to undertake this new assignment, because God's power was upon her as she pursued this task every day, totally submitted to His Will. Paul of Tarsus saw the social and spiritual intertwined, "Were you a slave when you were called? Don't let it trouble you—although if you can gain your freedom, do so. For the one who was a slave when called to faith in the Lord is the Lord's freed person; similarly, the one who was free when called is Christ's slave" (1 Corinthians 7:21–22).

Oleta's skills were vigorously sought after as word of her abilities spread over the Greater Indianapolis area. Reverend Lew Reynolds from the Sunday School Department of the Indiana Baptist Convention, was now asking her to assist in some of the Sunday School Workshops across the state of Indiana. Oleta had that burning desire to do God's Will. She boldly proclaimed, "I want to know the Lord's will and to have grace to do it, even if it results in sickness. Pray for me, that I may be a follower of Christ not in word only, but in deed and truth."

The summer Vacation Bible School was successful. The buses continued to bring in new children. We had refreshments, games, crafts, and Bible study everyday. At the close of VBS

Chapter 22 A New Challenge

we had a group picnic. With all that going on everyday in our church work, Oleta and I found that the hardest part of being missionary evangelists was to maintain a regular Bible and prayer time for ourselves. Even Jesus had to withdraw from the crowd to talk to the Father in Heaven.

Meanwhile, Barry and Jeffrey both attended the school just down the street from the church. It was just a nice walk from our house to the grade school. They seemed to be doing well in their studies and for that we were very thankful. Sibyl had completed all her work at Whiteland Community High School and was set for graduation on Friday, May 28, 1976, at 8:00 p.m. We all attended the exercises at the school and met many of our church members there. I preferred that Sibyl enroll at Cumberland College, Williamsburg, Kentucky, so I took her there for an interview and a look over the campus. Dr. James Boswell, the president of Cumberland College and a good friend of mine, was able to get her in the college in the fall of 1976. It was good to see so many of our youth in the community going on to college or some type of higher education. For all of this, we praised God and thanked Him from whom all blessings flow.

The year 1976 was a historic year for our American nation so we wanted to take our family to see some of the history of our nation. The Southern Baptist Convention was meeting in Norfolk, Virginia, June 15–17, 1976. We decided this would be a good opportunity to see places like Richmond and Charlottesville in Virginia, Philadelphia in Pennsylvania, and

Washington, D. C. We accomplished all of this as we motored to our meeting destination in Norfolk. While at Norfolk the children went to the beach and got a good sun tan too. I think Jeffrey got a little too much sun and nursed a sore back on the way home. Oleta and I attended a luncheon meeting sponsored by the Luther Rice Seminary of Jacksonville, Florida, now located in Lithuania, Georgia. I was greatly impressed about the Seminary and the dedication of the faculty to the Word of God. I commented to Oleta, as we left the luncheon meeting, that I would be a graduate of the Luther Rice Seminary someday.

There are not two Christ's, an easy-going one for easy-going Christians, and a suffering, toiling one for remarkable believers. There is only one Christ. Are you willing to abide in Him and bear fruit? Hudson Taylor, founder of the China Inland Mission, said, "We cannot do much, but we can do a little, and God can do a great deal." Psalm 37:4 promises, "Delight thyself also in the Lord, and he shall give thee the desires of thine heart." The boy from Back Creek said, "The Lord is prospering us and the work is steadily growing. In the stress and strain of the cold winter, it would be easy to forget our dream of God's work. The Lord cannot and will not fail us." The serenity of the Lord Jesus concerning any matter was the ideal base for the girl from 531 Pelham Street. She knew nothing of rush or hurry. She had no fear. There was always peace in her heart, a peace like that spoken of in Philippians 4:7, "And the peace of God, which passeth all understanding, shall keep your hearts and minds through Christ Jesus."

Chapter 22 — A New Challenge

I had longed for the opportunity to finish my theological seminary education and after meeting some of the faculty of Luther Rice Seminary at the Southern Baptist Convention in Norfolk, Virginia, I felt it was time to complete the master's degree. The Luther Rice Seminary in Jacksonville, Florida, had a correspondence course I could take. After transferring my theological work I had completed at Georgetown College and at the Southern Baptist Theological Seminary in Louisville, I could finish my degree and get my Master of Divinity in May of 1977.

I utilized the cold and snowy days of the winter as a good opportunity to do the work I needed to accomplish at some libraries and seminaries in Indianapolis. Oleta, my faithful companion, was ready to do my typing for the courses. In order to earn my degree, I had to write a lengthy thesis, which had to be approved by the Theological Committee at Luther Rice Seminary. I used the libraries often in gathering my material for the subject and I also used the Christian Theological Seminary's Library in Indianapolis. To substantiate my work, I perused many texts to obtain varied findings and views of others. An extensive bibliography had to be developed while numerous footnotes explained and gave further credence to my research. Since all this had to be done according to professional standards, I secured a typist in Indianapolis who did this type of work. I finally shipped my completed thesis to Luther Rice Seminary in Jacksonville, Florida. They accepted my work and bound the thesis in a book. The Luther Rice Seminary kept one copy and gave me two copies.

The Boy From Back Creek — James E. Casey, Jr.

My graduation day was scheduled for Friday, May 6, 1977 at 7:30 p.m. at the North Jacksonville Baptist Church, Jacksonville, Florida at 6415 Pearl Street. I purchased a round trip ticket out of Indianapolis to Jacksonville. Oleta drove me to the airport in Indianapolis and I was soon on my way. The Church was beautifully decorated for the commencement service. There were graduates there being awarded degrees at Bachelor, Master, and Doctoral levels. Dr. Robert G. Witty, President of Luther Rice Seminary, introduced the main speaker, Dr. Homer Lindsay, Sr., who was Pastor Emeritus of the First Baptist Church in Jacksonville, Florida. Dr. Robert G. Witty distributed the degrees. The benediction was given by a Nigerian student, Reverend David Jacobs.

I caught my return flight and Oleta was at the airport to meet me. I showed her the degree they gave her for putting me through this Theological training. Yes, she got the PHT degree, signed by the President just like mine. The PHT stands for Putting Husband Through. When I presented it to Oleta she said, "We have learned more lessons in faith than anything else because of our limited income."

A few weeks later Oleta and I were sitting and watching Lyndon graduate from Whiteland Community High School on May 20, 1977 at 8:00 p.m. The principal of the school asked that I give the benediction at the close of the program. Lyndon applied and was accepted as a student at ITT Technical Institute in Indianapolis. He drove the Plymouth Duster back and forth to the school and work. One day on the way back from school

Chapter 22 — A New Challenge

he got caught in a rain storm and had an accident. He did not get hurt but the car was damaged.

I think we human beings forget that the Bible is a written record and tells both the good and the bad in its historical narrative. When a Bible character does something devious, deceptive or down right dishonest, God is not putting His affirmation on it. He's simply recording it for us. The way Jacob treated Esau was wrong. Some of David's choices were not exemplary either. There were consequences for their actions, although they weren't always immediate. Jacob, the trickster, received a major trick from his manipulative father-in-law, Labon. Later, Jacob's sons tricked him into believing Joseph, whom they hated, was dead. Ultimately all these lessons molded Jacob into the man God designed him to be, but the process I am sure was painful, as it is for all of us who fail to obey God. There was one thing sure, Oleta and I had learned a lot since we first started out on this missionary journey. All of these years we have always tried to keep our sights on things above and to live every moment in the beauty of Christ.

In September of 1977 I was asked to be the guest speaker for the weekend at Swiss Colony Baptist Church, London, Kentucky. I was there to interview to become their pastor. Just about the time Oleta and I crossed the bridge into Kentucky, I looked around in the car and I did not have my Bible. Oleta looked up at me as if we had perhaps rushed out too quickly and it might be her fault. I told her not to worry. I was sure there would be a Bible at that hotel room. She was worried that

I needed the notes in my Bible. I told her that God would take care of everything. I simply put it all at the foot of the Cross. Could God provide in a difficult hour like this? Some people don't believe God will take care of them. Yes, God can provide! Yes, God is still in control. I was not worried. The girl I married had learned, since she walked up hollows and across footbridges in Eastern Kentucky, that the indwelling Christ in her life was still in control.

That was a blessed weekend. Joy filled both of our hearts as we headed back toward the Hoosier state. The next Sunday, I presented my resignation as pastor of First Southern Baptist Church effective on October 31, 1977. My work there was accomplished. There were other roads to travel.

Billy Graham was in Cincinnati, Ohio in an area–wide Crusade, October 24–28, 1977. I had the opportunity to be with the team and go to conferences during the day and participate in the Crusade at night. Fortunately I was able to do this before I left Indiana.

My last Sunday in New Whiteland was rather difficult because our family had planted deep roots in that community. We would leave Lyndon there because he was attending school in Indianapolis. The thing uppermost in my mind was the truth of the Gospel had been planted all over that community. It had been a blessing to serve our Lord in this great work. Our largest accomplishment was the knowledge that cold and indifferent men, women, boys and girls, who were once timid, were now boldly talking about Jesus Christ.

Chapter 22 A New Challenge

By October 31, 1977, our progress report on the First Southern Baptist Church showed that during our tenure total membership in the church increased to seven hundred fifty-nine. Additions from September 14, 1974 through October 31, 1977 totaled one hundred sixty-eight. The church properties, daycare and kindergarten were in functional order. The bus ministry was operating successfully. All church departments were functioning.

Chapter 23

Return To Kentucky

The Swiss Colony Baptist Church is located just outside of London, Kentucky, on Route 80 East toward Somerset, Kentucky. The church is rich in history of the Swiss people who came to Laurel County and began a wonderful community. The church sent a professional moving company to move us to our new residence in sight of the Baptist Church. The church parsonage was a two–story house. Jeffrey and Barry occupied the upstairs, while Oleta and I were on the first floor. Our washer, dryer, and freezer were located in the basement. It was a very nice house and was recently painted. We had a wonderful large yard which made a great playground for sports. I put my name on our mail box, which was down by the road in the front of the house. Our address was Route 2 Box 313, London, Kentucky 40741.

When Oleta and I were introduced in the Laurel River Association, we found it to be one of the sweetest fellowships we had ever been a part of in Kentucky. The Associational Director of Missions was Reverend Billy Wright. He and I soon were bonded together in such a way that it continued after I left that area.

I was always sensitive to what was going on in the community where I was pastor. When anything was not healthy for the community, I would speak out boldly on my disapproval. Sometimes that meant putting my life on the line.

I stood against the open sale of alcohol and was a war horse against the evils associated with it.

Oleta found friends in this move that have stuck with our family to her final day. Teaching children in a Sunday School class or a Vacation Bible School was always a part of her calling. She no longer depended on the hectograph, but quickly turned to a mimeograph machine, which made nice, clear copies for her class work.

Oleta and I worked with the existing programs that were in place for the first Christmas. The youth of the church were responsible for getting a live Christmas tree and decorating it. The church made a good Christmas treat available to every boy and girl who attended Sunday School. In addition, Reverend Delbert Binder, a member of the church, and I gave away a nice Christmas basket containing various kinds of foods for families to use at Christmas time. The Swiss Colony Baptist Church did not want anyone on the church field to feel lonely or left out at this season of the year.

One Sunday morning I walked up to several men who were gathered in the back of the church and I said, "Does the church have a budget?" Keith Binder said they did not have a budget and that money is not a problem in this church. He went on to say that the church was going to furnish me with an almost new Chevrolet van. In addition, all the gas and expenses on the vehicle would be paid for by the church. His only request was that I drive it and fill up the empty seats and win the unsaved in this community. I never asked again about a church budget and

Chapter 23 — Return To Kentucky

I drove the church van by the help of Almighty God as long as I was the pastor.

Jeffrey and Barry really did like the wide–open space in this country side. I went to Sears, Roebuck, and Company in London and ordered a go–cart for them to ride and play with on the church property. It developed some mechanical problems and they both agreed, that we should return it to the dealer. That ended the go–cart fun and perhaps prevented some bumps and sores on the boys' bodies.

One day shortly after the turn of the year in 1978, I entered my home in mid–morning when Oleta started talking about how open and friendly the people were here in Laurel County. I could see she was as happy as a robin redbreast chirping in the spring sun. Somehow I never did forget what Oleta had written me on January 29, 1957, as I was going into the mission field in Pike County, Kentucky. She wrote, "Jim, I have felt for a long time that is where you will be happiest." Of course, at that time she was referring to the Pike County mission field, but being back in Kentucky brought back those same feelings and memories.

Now about twenty years later both of us, after being in the great north of Indiana, were happy together in this field God had so wonderfully opened up to us and our family. We praised His Dear Name! AMEN!

We asked Reverend Billy Wright to be our teacher in the study of the book of Exodus. He did a wonderful job unfolding God's word to our people. We were seeing a lot of new people coming to Sunday School and the worship services. The church van was picking up several new people, especially boys and girls and some of whom were not Christians. We had several church members who were sick and needed a visit by the pastor. This was a concern of the church deacons and an effort was made by the pastor to take some deacons out on the house–to–house visitation.

God put in our hearts to visit one of our own church members. He was a war veteran and had been to the Veterans Administration hospital, who diagnosed he had cancer and gave him six months to live. We went to his bedside and read God's Word to him. We shared Matthew 7:6–11 and then 1 John 5:14–15. Each deacon prayed at his bedside and asked God to lift him up out of that bed and heal his body. It took a while for all of us to pray. But when we finished we felt God had moved on the scene. God is still in the healing business. One deacon, as we left, quoted part of Psalm 103:3, "Who healeth all thy diseases." The man lived for ten more years. AMEN ! PRAISE GOD!

When revival comes to the church body, the unsaved and unreached will take note of what is happening among God's people. Some people I visited were unsaved; they were slipping into eternity with all brakes on and still skidding. There were those who I visited that didn't drink booze or do a lot of other wicked things. They only had left Jesus out of their life. However, they were defeated, frightened, and wrecked by sin.

Chapter 23 — Return To Kentucky

The WMU promoted the Annie Armstrong Easter Offering for Home Missions and was thrilled by the response. God's hand was in it. With deep Christian commitment, Oleta would not give up until she had done her best to tell someone about Jesus. Oleta was an optimistic achiever. She dreamed great dreams and saw visions of what the ladies of the church could do in this community. She was a voice for all good causes and a teacher of the first order.

Vacation Bible School at Swiss Colony Baptist Church also brought in several new children. The church van travelled several routes in order to get as many children into the VBS as possible. There were a lot of other Baptist activities going on throughout the summer. There were Royal Ambassador camps at Cedarmore Baptist Assembly, Bagdad, Kentucky, and a Sunday School leadership conference at Ridgecrest Baptist Assembly, Ridgecrest, North Carolina.

I had received a 16mm film of *The Gospel Road*, a film made in Israel by Johnny Cash. We showed it at the Swiss Colony Baptist Church one Saturday night at 7:00 p.m. In addition, the ministers in the area were responsible for a religious radio program at 9:45 a.m. every Sunday over a radio station in London. I did this program several times and it was a great help in getting out God's word.

The State Missions Week of Prayer and Eliza Broadus Offering for Kentucky State Missions was September 10–17, 1978. The WMU was doing all they could to reach the Church goal for the offering. The following month, our church held a

Fall Harvest Revival from October 15–20, 1978. I had several Chapel programs at Sue Bennett College in London, Kentucky. Thanksgiving was observed with the attention of people drawn toward Almighty God. Closing the year, the Week of Prayer for Foreign Missions and the Lottie Moon Christmas Offering were observed December 3–10, 1978. Our congregation had been alive with activities in the Lord's name.

While our family was decorating the Christmas tree at the parsonage, Oleta looked over at me and said, "Do you remember that little tree we had there at Phelps, Kentucky? We had two strings of popcorn that I had strung up on thread and one little present under the tree for Sibyl. That was all we had. Now we've got a big beautiful tree all decorated and presents under it for four children and you and me." Then she added, "God doesn't forget His promises." My encourager reminded me of what God told me, "If you will take care of My business, I will take care of you." She never insisted on trying to tell me what to do about God's work. She looked me straight in the eyes and said, "I know when you decide to do something in God's work, it is of God. I trust you." I could do nothing but kiss and hug my darling wife.

The Swiss Colony Baptist Church showed its love for God and people by helping several families with groceries and other family needs. Treats were distributed to children in Sunday School and everyone seemed glad for the expressions of love.

Another year was beginning and believing the great God of this world wants all people to be saved, we focused on Psalm

Chapter 23 — Return To Kentucky

2:8, "Ask of me, and I shall give thee the heathen for thine inheritance, and the uttermost parts of the earth for thy possession."

Reverend Joe Mobley, who lives on Hawk Creek Road, conducted several successful revivals at the Swiss Colony Baptist Church while I was pastor. He is a great person to accompany on visitations and loves calling on lost souls. The Home Mission Board asked me to go to Adrain, Michigan, as one of the guest missionary speakers in a World Mission Conference, which was held on May 6–13, 1979.

In June, the whole family went up to Indianapolis, Indiana, to see Lyndon graduate from ITT Technical Institute with an Associates Degree in Electronic Engineering Technology. Shortly afterwards he found employment with Rockwell International in Cedar Rapids, Iowa. Meanwhile, Jeffrey took the driver's training course at Laurel County High School and got his driver's license. On occasion, he drove back and forth to school.

One day I got word from a Baptist Church in Winder, Georgia, that they were interested in bringing a group from their church to Kentucky to do some Vacation Bible School work and conduct some Bible Clubs. The man, who I spoke with, asked a lot of questions about the Swiss Colony area and mentioned that his church was interested in summer mission work. He said they would take care of their own lodging and meals during their stay. I went before the church and explained the whole deal to the people. The church agreed to have them come and organize a Vacation Bible School as well as coordinate several Bible Clubs in our community. We set the date and they came by car, truck, and bus. It all worked out in a wonderful way. The church van was full every time it came in. Everyone seemed to have a good time. The Bible Clubs were small in attendance, but we met a lot of personal needs. When it came time to have the closing service of the Vacation Bible School, it was decided we would have it on Saturday. We started out with a picnic and games, and ended up inside for the closing rally. The church auditorium was filled with children. The parents and visitors sat in the balcony. It was a thriller from beginning to the climax. The effort resulted in reaching more children for Christ than any other program we had tried. Many people were impressed. It goes to show what can be accomplished when God's people work together in love.

The WMU did ministry in the local community visiting those who were sick and shut–in, as well as visiting those in the nursing home in London. Oleta's love for others perhaps shined its brightest as she went to the nursing home or to someone in the community who needed a spiritual visit. The courage and sacrifice she demonstrated as she quietly sought the needs of others and her confident manner did the insufferable.

The Laurel River Baptist Association held a World Mission Conference October 21–28, 1979. Our church participated in the week–long conference, which had a total of three hundred thirty–one people in attendance.

Chapter 23 — Return To Kentucky

On November 29, 1979, the Swiss Colony Baptist Church was the host church for the quarterly Laurel River Associational WMU meeting. It was well attended and the Mission program was well received by those present.

The Swiss Colony Baptist Church observed the Week of Prayer for Foreign Missions and the Lottie Moon Christmas Offering December 2–9, 1979. The Christmas season was a time of sharing baskets of food with many people in the community. The church provided a Christmas treat for all the Sunday School children.

Back in the summer of 1979 I began working on my Doctor of Theology degree from International Seminary of Plymouth, Florida. Fortunately they offered the degree by correspondence, which allowed me to continue the Lord's work and obtain my degree at the same time. The hardest part was writing three 20,000 word theses. I spent many long hours diligently researching and studying in preparation for each thesis. With the help and support of Oleta, I completed all three theses. All the hard work paid off, on January 15, 1980, I received by mail my Doctor of Theology degree.

It was a new year and I was as busy as ever, I had the opportunity to go to the Holy Land with a group of ministers January 15–27, 1980. It was a great trip and the guide who was with the group everyday was outstanding. It was a trip never to be forgotten. I returned home for the Regional Royal Ambassador Congress held at Swiss Colony Baptist Church on

February 14, 1980. There were people present from different parts of the state and it was a very helpful meeting.

Lyndon enlisted in the United States Navy in February of 1980. He came to see all of us and we wished him God's best as he entered the Navy. On March 10, 1980 there was an Associational Evangelism Conference in the Association. The spring revival was conducted by Reverend Larry Isaacs of North Carolina. His family roots were in Laurel County and many people came to hear him preach God's word. The revival opened Sunday March 23 and closed on Friday March 28, 1980.

Oleta had a passionate longing for the spiritual welfare of those she taught. As she visited and taught, she believed that nothing really and abidingly succeeds if it is not well with a person's soul. She would say, as she sat in someones home or talked with someone in a nursing home, every person needs a refuge when that hour comes, an hour you can not escape, an hour you can not evade. She wanted everyone with whom she associated to know for sure that he or she was born again and bound for the Promised Land.

For many years, I had a calling from Almighty God to serve as a Director of Missions in some Baptist Association. I went to the Mid–Western Baptist Theological Seminary at Kansas City, Missouri, and studied for a week. I took all the training I could find so I might meet the qualifications of that position. The Home Mission Board of the Southern Baptist Convention gave me their assistance in finding a position. I contacted Reverend

Chapter 23 — Return To Kentucky

Robert C. Jones, of the Kentucky Baptist Convention, Middletown, Kentucky, and he wrote me that there was a need in the Russell Creek Baptist Association in Greensburg, Kentucky, for a Director of Missions. The committee asked that I come to Greensburg, look over the area, and discuss with them their needs and future plans.

I drove to Greensburg in Green County, and discussed the whole deal with them. The Missions Department would pay part of the salary and the Russell Creek Baptist Association would pay the remainder. I would have to find my own place to live and open up an office in my home or some other place. It was agreed upon by both parties and I, by faith, accepted the position. There were many things that were not completely clear. However, I was ready and willing to move on faith. I knew from past experiences the conquering weapon for Oleta and me was faith. The Bible tells us in Hebrews 11:6, "Without faith it is impossible to please Him." And 1 John 5:4 says, "This is the victory that overcometh the world, even our faith."

I did not really understand how the whole thing would work out so I did not want to limit God by my unbelief. The Israelites could have never entered the Promised Land without faith. Jesus wishes us to just believe Him. I came back and discussed this entire deal with Oleta. She left the entire matter with me. So before my God, I committed to this, the biggest move I had ever made.

I went before the Swiss Colony Baptist Church congregation and read my resignation as pastor effective on

June 30, 1980. The congregation was in shock. People I had baptized, and families I had been with in sickness and death looked at me with tears in their eyes and wanted to know why I was leaving them and wondered what can they could do to keep me. I told them that in my heart I felt this was God's will. God's will should be my will. I don't understand it all. I am taking a three thousand dollar a year cut in salary. I don't even have a down payment for a house and I don't have any office equipment. I don't really know anything to do but just trust God. I am really starting from ground zero.

The people in the Adrian, Michigan, vicinity wanted me to conduct a revival April 21–27, 1980. I gave them my very best. I was there to help them spiritually. I urged them, men and women, boys and girls, to settle the great matter where they will spend eternity.

Our daughter, Sibyl, was attending Cumberland College and living in Williamsburg, which was located just south of Swiss Colony. She graduated on Saturday, May 10, 1980 at 8:00 p.m. People have always enjoyed Sibyl because she has a sweet personality and makes friends easily. This was helpful in acquiring a position at the Whitley County Health Department in Williamsburg.

The Southern Baptist Convention was meeting June 8–12, 1980, in St. Louis, Missouri. Oleta and I had not had much time together in some little bit, so I announced I would take my family and attend the Southern Baptist Convention this year.

Chapter 23

Return To Kentucky

Oleta and I had made so many friends in our walk with Jesus in Laurel County while doing His work among the people. A gentleman, in whose house I had been in time of illness and who was also the owner of an automobile dealership, heard we were going to the convention and he asked if I could come by and see him. When I went to see him, we talked and prayed about his health and his work at the car dealership. When I left he pressed into the palm of my hand a credit card and said to use it like it was my own on the trip to St. Louis. This was not the first time he had been that kind and sweet to me.

A few months earlier, at the same time my wife's mother lay dying in a hospital in Lexington, some of my good friends in Indianapolis had asked me to come up for a few days of preaching, visiting, and witnessing in their church. The gracious pastor had made all the arrangements and I could not let him and these good people down. The same man who owned the automobile dealership asked me to drop by the dealership and pick up a car to drive to the revival. God never fails. He keeps His promises.

While there Oleta's mother did die and I had to leave one night before the meeting was over. Lyndon was still in Indiana trying to finish up his studies at ITT Technical Institute. He drove his car to Mount Eden and picked up my father and mother and brought them to the Funeral in Maysville. We all gathered in Maysville and went down to the funeral home to view the body of Iva Lancaster. As I looked down upon her lifeless body in that casket, I remembered that quiet little talk I had with her personally before Oleta and I were married. Iva at that time was a member of the Nazarene Church and she was not as faithful as she should be to Almighty God. We talked about spiritual matters and I explained some scriptures in her hearing. Finally we prayed. Shortly after this she started going to Central Baptist Church, where Oleta and Daisy were converted and baptized, and soon she was baptized. She became a loyal church member and worker in God's vineyard.

I had to resign as chaplain in the Civil Air Patrol. I had been appointed as a chaplain in the Civil Air Patrol on June 1, 1979 with the rank of Captain. I was attached to the Kentucky Civil Air Patrol Unit in London. I enjoyed this opportunity to be in the Civil Air Patrol and I worked with them on several different projects.

Jeffrey was going to be a senior and Barry was going to be a junior at the time we moved. We wanted to have Vacation Bible School at Swiss Colony Baptist Church before we moved away. The church van picked up children all around the community and it was a blessed thing to see them under the instruction of Godly teachers. The church clerk said there had been eighty–eight new members added to the membership roll of the church during my time there as pastor.

As we were about to come to that last service at Swiss Colony Baptist Church, Oleta said, "There are still about us people who are dying from the lack of personal attention. In sight of this church building, there are people who cross our paths from day to day. Numbers of them are in large families and unless something happens soon, some may die without getting saved." I replied, "There is only one who takes life's tears and attunes them to the sweetest music, and His name is Jesus."

Chapter 24

Director Of Missions

We were preparing to move to Greensburg, so I began looking for a house. I read the newspaper of Green County and talked with citizens within the community. I finally found a nice house for us to move into and perhaps purchase. The owner seemed willing to make the deal. I had talked with members of the associational committee I had dealt with from the very beginning about the house. Now we were ready to move. The Association provided a mover in London to move us. Bright and early the van arrived at the house and we were ready.

Jeffrey and Barry packed their belongings upstairs, while Oleta and I got the two cars loaded. It just so happened Lyndon was home on leave for a few days from the Navy, so we had plenty of help and everything went well. It did not take long to arrive at the new house and the unpacking soon began. The boys were big now and we had plenty of help, so it didn't take us very long to unload the moving van. Our boys were able to handle their room.

After we got moved in I began thinking how I could make one room in the house into an office. However, things can change very quickly. The owner of the house gave us word he decided to sell this house to another buyer. Just as we were getting settled into our new house, we were going to have to move again. But where? This reminded me of the Israelites having to move because of the enemies. I looked around in several neighborhoods in the town to see if I could find another house. We needed to find another house as quickly as possible. I remembered Paul and Silas, in the sixteenth chapter of Acts, were forbidden by the Holy Spirit to preach in Asia. They tried to get into Bithymia but were not permitted. The tender, earnest heart which has no will of its own except to find the Lord's will, can know the will of God and can have the sweet clear leading of the Holy Spirit. We did not give up. We did not take it as defeat. Often people spend a lot of time trying to get God to put his approval and blessings on their own plans.

Back to the newspaper I began to search for another house. In a short amount of time I found a really nice house on Locust Street. It even had a garage, which I knew could be converted into an office.

I did not have enough money for the down payment on the house, so the Russell Creek Baptist Association voted to lend Oleta and me ten–thousand dollars interest free for ten years. When our family departed from Laurel County, a member of Swiss Colony Baptist Church had given us two–thousand five hundred dollars to help us get started in purchasing a home. We now had the means to make the purchase and we closed the deal at once.

One of Pleasant Ridge Baptist Church members had a good rubber–tire wagon that we used to move our possessions around the city to our new home. Several men from the church joined in to help us move. It was a beautiful day and these men did a splendid job. We praised God for everyone who had a part in the move.

As soon as we got moved into the house, I began to study the possibility of remodeling the garage into a functional office for my work. Oleta and I studied the Bible and prayed about it. We came to the conclusion, as we read the Book of Job, that hard times and trouble are God's way of getting man's attention.

After having to move twice in one month, we decided remodeling the garage would be our own project. Oleta and I would pay all the expenses for the associational office, since the house was ours. I bought all the materials and hired Walter and Frank Wright to do the labor. They did a wonderful job and it was soon finished. This was the first associational office in the Russell Creek Baptist Association.

The automobile dealer in London, Kentucky, who had been so extra special to us, had an office desk, a typewriter, and a cabinet delivered to our house.

Oleta and I had to figure out how to get some bookcases made and a much needed work desk and cabinet. When you start out on a limited budget, you have to figure out some way to get the job done. I was not a very good carpenter, but my father could build just about anything and he was used to working on a small amount of money. I talked to him over the telephone about what I had in mind and asked him if he would help me with the project. My father and mother could come for a visit and do the work too. I drove to Mount Eden and brought them back to our new house. They were glad to assist in the project.

I went to the lumber company and got the lumber we needed and the Association paid for it. My father and I drew up the simple plans and we were soon at work on the wooden bookcase. We made it strong so it would hold a lot of books. Once we got it completed, Oleta and my mother starting putting the first coat of varnish on the wood. After they finished that painting job, Oleta decided to paint the inside of the office door leading to the outside. She did such a super job that everyone who came around always marveled at the job she did.

Constructing the work table and cabinet was going to be the hardest part of the project. It needed to be ten feet long and about three feet wide. The top had to be strong enough to hold up a copy machine, a paper-folding machine, and other office equipment that would be needed. My father looked at the lumber we had and figured out just how he could make it with the lumber we had without going back to get some more. We had to put heavy braces in it and the top had to be smooth so one could move things around on it. We were able to finish the work table and cabinet with a nice one piece bottom floor. All of the wood would require several coats of varnish to have a nice smooth finish.

After the project was completed, we filled the cabinet with books and tracts. We were ready to announce our office was open. We decided to have a dedication service on October 5,

Chapter 24 — Director Of Missions

1980 at 2:00 p.m. and give Almighty God all the praise and glory for His wonderful provision. The keynote speaker was Reverend George Price, Pastor of the Greensburg Baptist Church.

At the annual Russell Creek Associational meeting of 1980, it was voted to accept the Missions Committee's recommendation of renting the office space in our house for one-hundred twenty-five dollars per month for the Director of Missions office, including utilities.

A second telephone line to the house was installed in the office and was set to ring in the main part of the house also. I told everyone I would be available any time, day or night. I did not announce any closing dates of the office.

The WMU quarterly meeting was at the New Salem Baptist Church. The work of this missionary organization is to keep the people informed about mission work.

Jesus had a compassion for the unreached and the people in need. He did not see them as just a number, He saw them like sheep who needed the care of a shepherd. He was concerned for their comfort and so He had them sit down. He was concerned about their body, so He healed them. He was concerned about their spiritual needs so He warned them about hell. (See Matthew 18:8–14). This was what the Girl from 531 Pelham Street had surrendered her life to do and now she was here in an Association where there was so much work to be done for Christ. "The Master is calling." as she'd say to the ladies, "Grab hold of Christ's hand and go to work."

Meanwhile, I was busy trying to make contact with every pastor and church I could possibly work into my schedule. The Green County High School had begun. Jeffrey and Barry had to walk up the hill and across a few streets to the high school.

The Pleasant Ridge Baptist Church, located on Highway 88, asked me to help them in a revival meeting September 28, 1980 through October 5, 1980. We had an average attendance of about seventy-eight people per service for the revival. The Reverend O. D. Cooper, Pastor of Charity Baptist Church out from Columbia, Kentucky asked that I come and help him in a Revival Meeting October 13–19, 1980 and I thought it was a wonderful experience. The people generally filled the sanctuary every service. We did a lot of home visitation in the church field. Each service, we had an average attendance of fifty-four people. I attended the ordination of Wilburn Bonta into the Gospel Ministry at New Salem Baptist Church at 2:00 p.m. Sunday, November 30, 1980. He would pastor the Greasy Creek Baptist Church on Route 68 toward Edmonton, Kentucky.

Mrs. Bonnie McCloughn served as the Associational secretary and did the work from her home. I took the assignments to her home and returned for the completed work. She also did the monthly bulletin that went out in the mail. She was willing to do any secretarial work I asked of her. She was a blessing to me as she knew much about the events of the Association in past years.

Chapter 24 — Director Of Missions

There was a Minister's Association in Greensburg and I attended those meetings. This group sponsored a community-wide Thanksgiving service, where the attendance was very good. The Russell Creek Baptist Association had a Christmas banquet for the pastors and wives on December 2, 1980. This was an effective way to keep communication bonds among the pastors at large.

This was the first Christmas I was not serving as a Baptist pastor. Many people had told us that being a Director of Missions was a lonely position. Oleta and I both missed that close, warm fellowship of the church, but in our hearts we knew this new position was God's place for us. Yet, being a leader over a large region was tough and extremely difficult to cope with at times. There seemed to be no peers who really understood the load you carried. Then we unraveled the problem. We just did what God's word said in Matthew 11:28–30 and found Jesus' wonderful peace. Oleta said, "That's what Christmas is all about anyway—Peace."

The angels in Luke 2:14 proclaimed, "Peace, good will toward men."

Encouraged, we gathered around our decorated tree and shared what God had done for us. We praised Him for His marvelous grace and protection. I concluded, "We have so much. Yet, there still are people unreached and unsaved. That is why we are here. Let's pray that in some way we can do more for Jesus next year."

The 1981 year kicked off with the Russell Creek Executive Board Meeting held at Bethlehem Baptist Church and hosted by Pastor Reverend Gary Ervin. The moderator Reverend Michael Watts, pastor of Columbia Baptist Church, called the meeting to order. As Director of Missions for Russell Creek Baptist Association, I was asked to preach a tent revival held July 20–26, 1981 at property near the Bethlehem Baptist Church. Brother Irwin Milby, Jr. was heading up the event.

The Executive Board of the Association approved the purchase of a copier for the Associational office. There was an increased involvement by more people in the Associational meetings. The WMU was leading the way in getting ladies involved in Mission activities. The New Hope Baptist Church held the first Vacation Bible School in its history. They enrolled forty-four during the week of Vacation Bible School. Randy Milby was enthused about the youth meetings and planned on reaching more youth.

The annual Associational Meeting of the Russell Creek Baptist Association showed that two churches were admitted to the Association. The two churches were the Sparksville Missionary Baptist Church in Sparksville, and the Bethany Baptist Church near Columbia.

After being in the Russell Creek Baptist Association a little over one year, I observed that some churches on the Associational roll participated very little in the activities of the Association. I had a burden and broken heart for them as I saw so many people in need of a personal saviour. As an evangelist minister, my emphasis always targeted the unsaved. At Associational meetings I frequently referred to local people dying from the lack of a personal visit to their house. I further noticed that in sight of some of our church houses, there were people who needed to be saved. I challenged people to put Psalm 126:6 in practice. I taught that there are many ways to tell the Gospel story in your neighborhood.

We closed out 1981 in the Russell Creek Association with a Pastors and Wives Banquet at the Golden Corral Restaurant in Campbellsville, Kentucky. As our family gathered for the Christmas 1981 event at our house, we praised God for a wonderful year in His Vineyard.

I did not know when I moved to Green County and started working as the Director of Missions for Russell Creek Baptist Association that eventually I would also join with East Lynn Baptist Association as their Director of Missions too. It was Reverend Robert C. Jones who told me that if I could create a fellowship with the East Lynn Baptist Association, perhaps they would accept me as their director. That's exactly what I did. I attended their annual meeting and spoke to their people. A fellowship was created and the East Lynn Baptist Association asked me to consider being their Director of Missions along with Russell Creek Baptist Association. They were one hundred percent in favor of my doing what I could. I accepted the position with them and reported all that was happening in Russell Creek Baptist Association. Everyone was happy about this merger and I notified all those concerned that

I would begin my ministry with East Lynn Baptist Association on January 1, 1982. There were ten churches scattered in different counties in the East Lynn Baptist Association.

There were forty churches on record in Russell Creek Baptist Association. That meant I would now be working as Director of Missions, with a total of fifty churches.

After sharing this information with Oleta, she reminded me that when we were at Wheelwright I preached three times every Sunday, and before we married I preached four times each Sunday. With this new job I was going to be busy seven days a week. Psalm 37:7 says, "Rest in the Lord, and wait patiently for Him."

Russell Creek Baptist Association was starting off with a bang. A big youth valentine banquet was planned February 13, 1982 at the Deposit Bank at 6:00 p.m. in Greensburg.

Following close, the Bible drill and youth speakers tournament was to be at New Salem Baptist Church on February 26, 1982 at 7:00 p.m. The East Lynn Baptist Association planned a big evangelism rally at Mount Carmel Baptist Church with Reverend Joe Mobley of London, Kentucky, as the keynote speaker. The Holly Grove Baptist Church notified us they were hosting a Sunday School rally on May 7, 1982 at 7:00 p.m.

The Russell Creek Baptist Associational WMU invited Brother Randal Moore as guest speaker. The Girls in Action and Acteen's had a fantastic track meet. The Russell Creek and

Chapter 24 — Director Of Missions

East Lynn Baptist Associations both had very good annual meetings. It seemed like God's work was making progress in both Associations. Churches were encouraged by the abundant and varied activities. The East Lynn Baptist Association had a Ministers and Wives Banquet at the Golden Corral Restaurant in Campbellsville on December 2, 1982, at 7:00 p.m. The Russell Creek Baptist Association held a Christmas Banquet for all pastors and wives at the Deposit Bank in Greensburg on December 3, 1982 at 6:00 p.m.

The Director of Missions closed the year 1982 with thanksgiving for all the churches and the blessing to serve God in this mission field.

As 1983 began the East Lynn Baptist Association was sending one hundred dollars each month to the Russell Creek Baptist Association to help with office expenses in God's work in the Association.

There was a great need for people and the churches to be more concerned about reaching the lost and those not attending any Gospel church. If we were going to be Missionary Baptists, we needed to follow the instructions of Matthew 28:19–20 and Acts 1:8. We must show our concern for all souls, both black and white. A Baptist rally was conducted at Bethlehem Baptist Church with Reverend Paul Lambert and Reverend John W. Smith as speakers. The meeting proved to be very valuable and caused many people to turn from sin and get saved. The Week of Prayer for State Missions and the Lottie Moon Christmas Offering for Foreign Missions was a concern as the WMU focused on missions and reaching people with the Gospel message. WMU ladies believed if you neglect missions, then you were leaving out the heart of the Bible.

The South Summerville Baptist Church, pastored by Reverend Jerry Noe, was admitted to the East Lynn Baptist Association in 1983. Early in 1984 the Green Hill Baptist Church of Greensburg, was admitted to the East Lynn Baptist Association. Reverend Carlos Compton was the pastor.

The missionary spirit flared as two of our men from Russell Creek Baptist Association were engaged in overseas mission work. Mr. Randall Rogers went to India and Reverend Doyle Searcy was commissioned to work in China. Two of our churches in Russell Creek Baptist Association helped with the Korean work at Radcliff, Kentucky. Brush Creek Baptist Church had burned and they entered into a building program. The congregation soon constructed a new sanctuary which was dedicated to God. The East Lynn Baptist Association held a Sunday School meeting at Holly Grove Baptist Church with about two hundred people present.

This was a difficult year for the boy from Back Creek and the girl from 531 Pelham Street. Medical doctors in Campbellsville discovered that Oleta had cancer in the right breast. Everyone is different and everyone deals with serious illness in his or her own way. What to do? After the diagnosis, Oleta and I decided to take the doctor's advise. The closing hours before Oleta submitted to the operation were frightening. I cancelled all of my out of town engagements. I wanted to be right there with Oleta. I tried to stay calm and explained to people that everything would be all right. Oleta and I were relieved to hear that the doctor who was in charge of the surgery was one of the best in our area. On the day the surgery was scheduled, we both were in deep prayer about the surgery. We were settled in our hearts that this was absolutely the right path to follow, even if it was unnerving. However, Bible study and prayer convinced us that we should keep our faces toward Almighty God. We got to the Taylor County Hospital in Campbellsville on time and everything was in place for the surgery. When it was time for Oleta to go in for all the preparations, I kissed her and whispered a prayer for her as they quietly took her away to that cold room.

A nurse told me that when it was over, the doctor would come out and let me know how it went. I was told about how long the surgery would take. When that time came for it to be over, I was a little nervous, sitting there all by myself. When the doctor did come through the door, I could tell by the look on his face, it was a big success. Then he put his arm around my shoulder and told me exactly how the surgery went. Yes, he got it all and as far as humanly speaking every thing should be alright. I knew then that the Master above had visited the scene and our prayers had been answered. In a few days Oleta was sent home from the hospital. Sure she had to return to the doctor's office after so many days, but the trip was just to make sure all was going well. Even after a month or so, she was asked to see the doctor ever so often to keep a check on how things were going. This continued as long as we lived in

Greensburg. However all tests always showed there was no trace of any cancer. The good doctor and his staff had done their job. The Father in Heaven, also had done His job.

The spirit of enthusasm continued in both Associations. The youth in East Lynn had a revival and it netted four saved and one rededication. A large Sunday School rally in East Lynn drew the attention of several people. The brotherhood in Russell Creek had one hundred men for a morning breakfast. Again East Lynn drew two hundred people out for a Sunday School rally at Holly Grove. Both associations had record crowds at their annual meetings. The Russell Creek Baptist Association voted to study a Mission project in Enterprise Baptist Association.

Oleta looked around at the progress of the various projects in both associations and pointed out that there was a lot of excitement about God's work in these two associations. I told her that God was doing a mighty big thing in a lot of people's lives. Oleta told me she read in one of her Christian magazines that success and failure are relative to time and place, but for those who love and seek to be in the center of God's will, all of life is a success. This was our fourth Christmas in Green County. I was happy in the Associational work. I read in the Bible that called people should "fight the good fight of faith." (See 1 Timothy 6:12). We can follow Christ a far off, or we can walk beside Him, and be His conscious friend and worker. That's what was going on in these two associations;

people were lining up and walking with Jesus as the year came to a close.

It was a true spirit of love for Jesus and His work that drew people to the Associational Sunday School rallies in East Lynn Baptist Association. There were two hundred people present at the January 1985 meeting at Green Hill Baptist Church in Greensburg. Reverend Don Watson was the guest speaker. The Russell Creek Baptist Association finalized their plans to help churches in the Enterprise Baptist Association in revival work in the spring. Several groups were assigned places to serve. Reverend Larry Wisdom and I were assigned to go to Wheelwright. I was to preach and Reverend Wisdom was the song leader. There was a total of two hundred twenty-four people who attended the services.

The first Bi-Vocational Pastors and Wives Dinner was held for both associations on Friday March 27, 1985 at the Wilson Family Restaurant in Campbellsville at 6:30 p.m., with a total attendance of thirty-one. The East Lynn Baptist Association and Russell Creek Baptist Association voted to put their news letters in the Western Recorder, which is the state Baptist newspaper in Kentucky.

Because of her years of experience, Oleta was asked to help in the Associational Vacation Bible School Clinic. It was her gift of teaching children that took her to help the Sulphur Springs Baptist Church in their Vacation Bible School. I was the Director of the Vacation Bible School. The New Hope Baptist Church also requested her service as a teacher at their

Vacation Bible School for several years. One day while driving to New Hope for the Vacation Bible School I told Oleta that we were going to have to furnish most of the supplies for this Vacation Bible School. She agreed and said, "If you preach Missions, then you are supposed to do it." We came to this Association on faith and we lived by faith. That was enough for both of us. This was the life of a diligent missions worker. She did not like sitting in an office and telling others what to do. She wanted to get her hands into it herself. Nothing thrilled her any more than telling children her story about God and His wonderful love.

The Leatherwood Baptist Church was a small country church and was quite a distance from Greensburg, but it was a place Oleta and I fell in love with. We got there one cold winter Sunday morning. The ground was still frozen when we drove up beside the church. We got out with our big winter coats on, walked over the frosty frozen ground and pulled open the front door. Inside there was a little warmth but not enough to remove our coats.

There was no one available to play the piano, but the song leader, a good man of God, looked at his watch and said it was time to get the service started. He cracked loose in his big manly tone on "When The Roll Is Called Up Yonder." He sang loud and clear. There were just six of us at service, but all six sang because this man who was leading us knew where he was going. Yes, you could tell by the look in his eyes and the joy in his voice. Next the song leader asked the other man who was there, who happened to be his brother, to pray. You should have heard his prayer. This man had no theological training, but the way he spoke to God in prayer told us he was no stranger to Jesus. The song leader then took that song book *Voice of Praise*, compiled by B. B. McKinney, and flipped it open to page thirty-four. We all stood and sang "The Old Rugged Cross." He didn't stop until all four stanzas were sung with mounting volume. After the last stanza he picked up a little black offering plate, dropped in some folding money and said, "If you got some money you want to give to the Lord, put it down here." Turning to me and Oleta, he thanked us for coming all the way from Greensburg and asked me if I wouldn't mind coming up front and preaching.

I went to the front of the church, still wearing my overcoat and overshoes, and began to preach. I already felt good down in my soul. I knew these four people had come to church that day to hear from God's word. I turned to Luke's Gospel, Chapter 16, and read verses nineteen through thirty-one. It was a cold winter day, but I spoke on the "Horrors of Hell". I told them hell was a real place. It was a place filled with suffering and if you go to hell you can't get out. I closed by saying the reason God sent Jesus to this earth was to keep people out of hell. I asked that we stand and sing, "Amazing Grace," number one hundred sixty-one in the *Voice of Praise* hymn book.

The song leader thanked us for coming and asked me to come back and preach some more. The song leader's brother and his wife said some kind words to Oleta and me, then handed me some money and told Oleta and me to go into Edmonton and eat a good meal. I handed the gift to Oleta and we walked out to the car, got in, and drove toward Edmonton. As we made our way out that little narrow road that led to the Church, Oleta said I should have refused the gift because we didn't deserve to eat with their money. I told her that we didn't come here for a free meal, it came from a heart of love. We talked as I drove and at times little tears came to both of our eyes about people who live this far out in the country. They really love Jesus!

I thought back to the time on Back Creek when Reverend Foster E. Howard befriended my dad and turned my family around. I told Oleta that was why we came out to this little church. God had called us here and we can't forget these little churches. These little churches mean a lot to the six or eight who attend. I was so glad we were able to witness that again here today. I would just as soon be here as in the big First Southern Baptist Church in New Whiteland, Indiana. I wasn't out for the money and my wife learned that years ago. We got into Edmonton and went straight to the little country restaurant we had visited before.

We were hungry because we had been up ever since 6:00 a.m. The food was good, but Oleta just could not get over worshipping with her winter coat and overshoes on and me standing up there preaching with overcoat and overshoes on. She said that when God made me he must have broken the mold, because there wasn't anyone else like me. As we drove

Chapter 24 — Director Of Missions

back to our house, Oleta just gazed out the car window. When we drove into Greensburg I thought to myself, Oleta and I have so much to learn about Jesus' Promise to quench that thirst we both have for Him.

I had put in writing and I told people verbally that I would come and visit with them on their church field. One pastor took me up on that offer. He told when and where to meet him, and we would visit on his church field. When I got there he was waiting and had a list of people for us to visit.

As we approached a house, the pastor explained that it belonged to a ninety–two year–old–man who would not listen to what anyone told him about the Bible or Jesus. Inside the old man's house we found him sitting near his big potbelly stove. I approached him and we talked about things in general. Finally, I asked if he would mind if I read from the Bible and say a prayer before we left. The old man said it was alright, so I read from John 3:16, John 3:36, and John 14:1–6. I continued, after getting his approval, reading from Romans 10:9–13. I told him a little about confessing and believing in Jesus. Then I said, "Have you ever believed in your heart and confessed with your mouth Jesus as your personal Savior?"

He said, "No I ain't done nothing like that."

I stepped closer to the man and read Ephesians 2:8–9, Revelation 3:20, and finally 1 John 1:9. I looked him straight in the eye and said, "Would you like to go to Heaven when you die?"

He replied, "I guess it would be a good thing."

I pressed on, "God is knocking at your heart right now and if you will let Him in, He will forgive your sin and take you to Heaven when you die."

Then I said, "Let's bow our heads and pray, and you ask Jesus to come into your heart and forgive your sins."

We both bowed and I led in a prayer. When we finished, I said, "Did you ask Jesus to come into your heart?"

He replied, "Sure did, preacher."

I gave him the assurance, "If you asked Him, then He is in your heart."

What do you think? I believe He is in the old man's heart. We left and the pastor baptized the ninety-two year-old-convert the next Sunday. I saw the pastor some time later and he informed me that the old man lived about six more weeks and then suddenly died. It does pay to visit. Psalm 126:6 NIV says, "Those who go out weeping, carrying seed to sow, will return with songs of joy, carrying sheaves with them." Let us all do our very best as it could be the last visit for someone.

A World Mission Conference was planned for Russell Creek and East Lynn Baptist Associations for October 6–13, 1985. The Russell Creek Baptist Association had a youth meeting with one hundred young people attending. The youth raised five thousand dollars to build Churches in Kenya, Africa. The word Missions was catching on in God's work. The East Lynn Association had recently sent one thousand dollars to build two churches in Kenya, while the Allendale Baptist Church had sent five hundred ten dollars to build a church in Kenya.

That's the way we closed out the year 1985, just praising His dear name and thankful for a little place to serve Him on planet earth.

Chapter 25
Mission Trips Abroad

My first trip to Israel was in 1980. I went with a group of ministers from various places across the United States of America. I believe it was perhaps one of the most learning experiences I have ever been on in my entire life. The guide was so knowledgeable of the entire countryside, that he made it come alive as we journeyed with him day by day. He provided much insight into the places like Hebron, Masada, Bethlehem, Nazareth, Meggido, Jericho, Jerusalem, Tiberias, Betheny, and many more. We could see that this countryside was beginning to come alive under the leadership of the Jewish people.

During my travel to Israel, I got a deeper understanding of the Jewish people as we traveled to Qumran and Masada. We drove through the Judean desert into the Jordan Valley, then on to Jericho where we were told how this old city was destroyed in the days of Joshua. A little farther south we stopped at Qumran and viewed the caves where the Dead Sea Scrolls where found. We motored on to Masada, where we ascended by cable car to the top of a mountain, to visit Herod's mountain bunker and the last stronghold of the Jewish revolt against Rome (66–73 A.D.). We were shown where the Jewish people stored water and other supplies on top of this mountain. We walked down the backside of the mountain and viewed the ramp built by the Romans. At the top of the mountain, we saw where the Romans broke through the wall that the Jews had built to keep out the enemy.

God had been good to the boy from Back Creek and the girl from 531 Pelham Street. In April of 1985, I went on my second trip to Israel following in the steps of our Savior., but this time Oleta went with me. We decided now would be a good time for both of us to see the Holy Land. We travelled with a group which was mostly Baptist tourists. Our spiritual leader was able to read from the Bible as we journeyed from day to day. We discussed the footprints of Jesus as we travelled the route He took during His public ministry on earth.

After we moved to Florida, once again the Lord moved us to go to Israel. Sibyl was able to go along this time. The other trips went out of J.F.K. airport in New York but this time we departed from Newark, New Jersey. The trip lasted from March 17 to March 26, 1999. It was a good trip across the ocean, and everyone on board seemed to enjoy the ride. We stayed in several cities in Israel. On this trip we went to some places neither Oleta nor I had seen—like the Baptismal Pool on the Jordan River and Beth Shean where King Saul was killed in battle.

In the Holy Land one can see where Jesus was born, lived, ministered, crucified, and then ascended back to Heaven. All of this drew us closer to Almighty God, and we were never the same after such an experience. Being in the Holy Land let us know personally that God's Word has not changed and neither have His plans changed. (See Malachi 3:6). Because God has

Chapter 25 Mission Trips Abroad

no beginning and no ending, He can know no change. Because He has not changed, He can still give you peace in troubled times.

After being in the Holy Land, the Girl from 531 Pelham Street was more determined to lay it all on the altar for Jesus. She, even in retirement, spent long hours in the Master's work. To her, the Rapture could be any moment and she wanted to be busy in His Kingdom Ministry somewhere on earth.

Reverend Robert C. Jones, of the Kentucky Baptist Convention, asked Oleta and me if we would like to go to Kenya, Africa for a Mission trip November 28, 1985 to December 15, 1985. We left with the group, and Oleta, anxious for the opportunity, fell into visiting, witnessing, and soul winning just like she did in America. We were together, hand in hand, in the tribal huts, and down by the riverbanks walking, talking, and preaching. Oleta fell in love with the youth and children and their great love for Jesus. Neither of us, when we said those marriage vows in 1957, ever thought we would hold hands in Kenya, tell people about Jesus, and see them baptized as followers of Jesus Christ.

We experienced many rainy days during the trip to Kenya. One day a missionary took us way out in the back woods where the few roads were mud roads. Finally we reached the place where we were going to teach and preach. The culmination was an all night church service of singing and testifying. Oleta worked with children and youth. She used her talents now in the heart of Kenya and the children and youth flocked around to hear her voice and see her beautiful smile.

I did some preaching during the day. People walked from afar. They crossed and waded through water to get to the places where I was preaching. It was a joyful time for those people to come and worship the living God. We ate with them and had a good time fellowshipping together. At night they really seemed to get excited about singing, testifying, and praising the Lord.

They planned to stay all night and let God have the glory and praise. Oleta and I wanted to stay all night but about midnight the missionary told us it was time to go home or we would not be able to do anything tomorrow. The missionary said he knew a short cut through this back country, so we took off through a dark wooded place. The road was narrow with deep cut tracks in the mud about a foot deep. It was raining hard, but the automobile was doing very well in this mud and driving rain.

Somewhere out there in this backwoods area, the automobile began to slow down and eventually stopped. The missionary explained that the vehicle had drowned out. He got out, raised the hood and began to wipe off the motor with a small piece of cloth he found in the automobile. When he got back in the automobile and tried to start the motor, it did not make a sound. The only light we had was a small flashlight. It was very dark as the trees hung over this little narrow road. The missionary warned us that this was not a very safe place to spend the night as there were roving bands of bandits in the area. He did not feel comfortable letting us sit there all night.

As we sat there, each of us prayed the motor would get dry enough to start. After about thirty or forty minutes the missionary said he would try it again. He got out in that deep mud and wiped some more on the motor to dry it off. With mud up to his knees, he got back in the automobile and the motor finally started. He let the motor warm up for a while, then he asked me to get out and push the automobile so we could get out of there. I got out in the mud and gave my best in pushing the automobile. It soon moved forward and we got out of that dreadful place. It was about 2:00 a.m. when we arrived at the missionary's home. Oleta and I cleaned up and went to bed, thanking God for taking care of us.

By 10:00 a.m. that day, we were ready to go back to the campgrounds where the all-night service had been held. When we arrived, most of the crowd was gone but we did have a Gospel Service before we left. We made other stops at places where few white people had ever been. They looked over the boy from Back Creek and the girl from 531 Pelham Street real good. They just wanted to touch a white person. So we did stop and walked over to those who just wanted to touch us. The little black boys and girls came up and touched our white skin. They giggled and laughed, then darted back away from us. It was an experience for us as well as it was for them. The whole village was so shaken by this unusual experience, they darted in from all directions to see the white people who had come to visit them.

We took out the portable mike system and set it on top of the automobile and told them about Jesus. Helpless now and astonished, the people grew quiet as I talked about Jesus. My message was brief, but to the point. God had kept his Promise to the girl from 531 Pelham Street and the boy from Back Creek. He let us carry the Good News of Jesus to a land that knew nothing about Him, until we stood there and spoke the words of Jesus to them. As Oleta walked away she said, "To God be the Glory." Then I said, "Praise the Lord one person got saved."

Oleta and I had learned at Phelps, Kentucky, what it was like to wholly trust God, because God is indeed enough. That is the secret by which we have lived and will live until He takes us Home to be with the Father in Heaven forever.

In the fall of 1991 I began to pray about going to Brazil on a Mission trip with some other Southern Baptists who were interested. I decided it would be a good thing if I joined this Mission trip to Brazil. It was set for November 14–21, 1991. I got my traveling bags ready and flew out of Louisville with the group of Southern Baptists. We changed airplanes in Miami, Florida and then flew to Rio de Janeiro, Brazil. Then we took a small plane on up to the site where we were going to work during the mission projects.

I preached several times to a crowd of people and there were several conversions. We helped finish up a church house

Chapter 25 — Mission Trips Abroad

for a small group of Baptist believers before we left. We assisted in visitation in some areas, which was very fruitful. Part of our work included feeding the homeless people in the area. Not far from where we were building the new Baptist church building, there lived about five thousand homeless people. They did not have a house of any kind. Some had a piece of plastic stretched over them, to cover some of their clothes. These people were of all ages, mothers with babies and small children, elderly men and women, the sick, the crippled, and those with absolutely nothing except what they were wearing.

We took food to them several days. They would form a line and march up with a cup or a piece of plastic and take what little food we had to offer them. The saddest part was the line grew longer every day and we only had so much food. One day the line was so long that our food did not cover all that big long line of human flesh. We dished a large spoonful to each person in line, hoping we could give everybody there at least one bite of food. I noticed an old crippled lady holding in her hand a piece of plastic to get her bite of food. Unfortunately, we were not able to feed everyone that day. Some were not able to get even one bite of food. I watched this old lady as she turned and walked away. I wondered what would happen to her.

We left Brazil with thoughts like this on our mind. Nothing much we could do. I wished and wished we could have done more. We flew back to the United States of America and I, for one, have not forgotten seeing that long line of homeless people.

While looking through the Western Recorder, the Kentucky Baptist Convention state paper, I read that Dr. James "Jim" Ponder, of Orlando, Florida, needed volunteers to go with him on a preaching crusade in Russia from June 23 through July 15, 1993. I told Oleta that I was going to sign up as a volunteer to Russia. She asked me where I was going to get the money. I said, "God has it; that's all I know."

Shortly after I signed up in February 1993 to preach in Russia, I had a severe pain in the stomach. I discreetly went to see my medical doctor, who took x–rays. It showed I had a large hernia in the stomach and it needed repairing immediately. I told the doctor of my plans to go to Russia in June. He recommended, rather sharply, that I should not travel unless the hernia was successfully repaired.

The operation was a success. I healed rather quickly and the plans to go to Russia were on schedule. I did all the things the doctor advised. It was now April and the doctor was carefully monitoring my progress and he believed I would heal completely in time to go to Russia. By the first of June I was ready to go. Our God in Heaven, has the power to do anything He chooses. However, over and over in the Bible, He permits things to happen to His people to test their faith.

Chapter 26
Director Of Missions Continued

The Russell Creek Baptist Association voted to have a Mission link up with Steel Valley Association in Ohio to do Mission work in 1986.

We had a sixteen inch snow the first week in February of 1986. Schools were closed and we cancelled anything we had scheduled in our Associational work. That same month the Russell Creek Association had twenty-two churches committed to the Good News America Revival and East Lynn Association had nine churches committed. The East Lynn Baptist Association recently had one hundred-fifty present for a Sunday School meeting. The Seminary Extension Project was very fruitful. I know of ten people who completed the study of the Book of John.

After serving six years in the U. S. Navy, Lyndon was honorably discharged in January 1986. He returned to Kentucky and was soon employed at the Commonwealth of Kentucky Department of Transportation in Frankfort.

The Russell Creek Baptist Association, at their Board Meeting, hired Oleta to do all of the Associational secretary work. The Whickerville Baptist Church was admitted to the East Lynn Baptist Association on April 5, 1988.

The Greensburg Baptist Church through its WMU organization was doing literacy work. Oleta used her training and knowledge in literacy to help people. This is often the unreported work because those in the program do not want to talk about it publicly.

The work of the Sunday School in our churches was growing. The Sunday School Growth Campaign in Russell Creek Baptist Association netted several new people brought to the churches for Bible study. In the East Lynn Baptist Association the rallies were held in different churches and brought out people by the droves with a total attendance running from one hundred fifty people to sometimes as high as two hundred people to hear God's man tell the old, old story of Redemption.

The Brotherhood Ministry in the Russell Creek Association was growing. One thing that kept the boys busy was the Royal Ambassador Racer Derby. There were eight men from Russell Creek Baptist Association who went on a Mission trip to Jamaica. The youth in Russell Creek Baptist Association were growing in their awareness of missions and doing the will of God. The Kentucky Sports Crusaders helped the youth a lot and brought large numbers to the Lord.

The Spirit of Revival was moving in the hearts of many people in both of the Associations. I had been in revival meetings in a great number of the churches in the Russell Creek Association and the East Lynn Association. In these revivals I meet all kinds of people. I remember in one revival, a couple explained that for two years the wife had breast cancer and it was in stage four. However, now through the goodness

Chapter 26 — Director Of Missions Continued

and mercy of God, the doctors say it is in remission. In another revival the pastor and I made an attempt to meet and talk with a seventeen year old boy. That night he was killed in a motorcycle accident. Yes, we saw him but he was in a casket.

Yet, in another revival, I was asked to talk with a young couple who had a small child, about six months old, about spiritual matters. In a few days, that young lady suddenly died in their own bedroom. Life is short, no matter how long a person may stay on planet earth. So I advise people to get right with God, and keep your eyes on Jesus no matter where you live. I tell people He will take you safely to the other shore.

Through the years, I had several discipleship training sessions. I witnessed several people committed to a higher level of living. I have met several people who just don't want to pay the price of following close to the Lord. Yet Randall Rogers, who was a member of the Bethlehem Baptist Church, moved up closer to the Lord. A person must be willing to obey the Lord. The Bible says we are to obey the Lord. (See John 15:10 and John 14:21). Are you willing to read your Bible more?

What about loving others? (See John 15:12–17). Maybe you need to visit somebody and help them out. You see loving others is essential for you to grow as a Christian. (See John 15:8 and 1 Peter 4:8). The reason you are not enjoying your daily life could be you just have over looked the essentials.

In 1991 we had tremendous crowds attending the annual associational meetings. We had shortened some things but were determined to make the main thing—the Main Thing. I found out in church work you have to listen to the people. When I moved to associational ministry, I found out you still must listen to the people. In recent years, as our churches were moving to television and other electronic media, I told the brethren that the Gospel never does change. In my work I tried to keep the simple plan of Salvation the highlight for all—the Main Thing. Too often we get so busy with things that we don't pay attention to what we are supposed to be doing for Jesus. With Oleta as Associational secretary, she would always say, "I'm not doing this for pay, but for Jesus." Since the office was in the house, I saw her work many a night until past 10:00 p.m. No overtime pay. Just doing it for Jesus.

The year 1992 was such a rich and beautiful year. Oleta, now my secretary, was giving freely so much of her time to the Associational office. Even when I would ask her to report her hours, she would always turn the other way. I learned to just let her do it her way.

The year started out with the East Lynn Association Youth having a Lock–in at Campbellsville College and the WMU of Russell Creek Baptist Association having big success in their Ministry. The laymen were planning a summer weekend revival in the Russell Creek Association.

The youth of Russell Creek reported they had over one hundred in a youth rally. When I showed my slide pictures of Brazil, many asked to know how they could get involved in helping in the work in Brazil. We had softball games going for

Chapter 26   **Director Of Missions Continued**

boys in the summer. I saw where one hundred fifty had attended a big event at a local church.

In July of 1992 I reported that for the first time in a great long time all the churches in Russell Creek and East Lynn had a pastor. The annual meetings of both associations were well planned and went over with large crowds attending. By the end of July 1992 I had already visited every church in both Associations. Some I had visited four or five times. The churches were pleased when Oleta made and I passed out the 1993 calendars in October of 1992.

That relentless girl from 531 Pelham Street was committed. I really believe it was her deepest desire to know Christ better. If I ever mentioned giving up or quitting something, she did not want to listen to it. She often said in a quiet voice, "But Jesus would not quit." She believed Jesus was more real in His help to her than any other being in the world. Time and again she would say, "If I am to know Jesus better, I must be willing to pay the price to know Him." The last piece of work she ever did for the Russell Creek and East Lynn Associations, she did free. She read those words in Philippians 3:8 and she was willing to say, "I paid the price."

I haven't seen it all, but this boy from Back Creek has had the wonderful privilege of telling the story of Jesus Christ in many different places in this world. I was asked by the Home Mission Board to assist in an Associational Mission Conference early in my preaching ministry in a remote section of Eastern Kentucky. It was in the autumn of the year in the

The Boy From Back Creek   James E. Casey, Jr.

Appalachian Mountains of Kentucky and in the evening the mountains looked like a thousand rainbows descending on the hills and hollows of the beautiful mountains. It was raccoon and opossum hunting time in these mountains, but I was here to tell the people about the Lord Jesus Christ and what He could do for them and with them.

My preaching assignment one night was to a little Baptist church nestled way back on the other side of the mountain range. The gracious gentleman who guided me that night to my preaching point, started giving me instructions about this church as we drove thirty-five or forty miles to this Baptist church. This is what he told me to expect when we arrived at the church. He said they used coal oil lamps hung on the walls of the church building. He said the pulpit was home-made and a water bucket with a dipper was right there beside it. He also said there would be a coal oil lamp up there close to the pulpit so I could see to read from the Bible. He pointed out that they did not use song books but the folks all knew the songs. He also said the deacons usually sat on the right side of the church.

By the time my driver told me what to expect, we were pulling into the driveway that led to the little rustic frame Baptist church. I noted, as we passed the men and women walking and carrying lanterns towards the church, their hunting dogs were in front wagging their tails and occasionally barking. We got out and went inside the church building, but most of the men stayed outside chewing their tobacco. The song leader told me that when the men finished talking and chewing tobacco, it

Chapter 26 — Director Of Missions Continued

would be time to start the service. It wasn't long until the men filed in and took their usual places. The song leader began to hum that old Baptist hymn "When the Roll is Called Up Yonder" and the congregation soon joined in. They sang so loud and powerful that I thought the roof might shake loose. You could tell these folks had a real dose of salvation.

After we finished singing and praying, a gentlemen with bib overalls on got up and said, "I hear this good preacher has come a long way; let's turn him loose and see if he can preach." I got up and read Acts 1:6–9, and then I told them about God's great love for lost souls. My Sermon had these points :

- All have sinned (Romans 5:12)
- Jesus will save you. (John 3:16, 18, 36)
- Now is the time (Revelation 3:20, I John 1:9)

When I was about to finish a young mother, on the front seat, started breast feeding her six–week–old baby. For a moment I didn't know who was going to get the most attention. However, I soon called for the song leader to come forward and lead us in the hymn "Amazing Grace" and the service closed. When it was all over the men and women all wanted me to come back and preach to them some more.

As my driver and I drove back to my place where I was staying, I thanked Almighty God for the privilege to tell people about Jesus Christ. Yes, I have had a heap of living on planet earth, but I must be honest and tell you that right here in

Greensburg, Kentucky, are some of the sweetest people in the world.

As I made my rounds through Greensburg, I mentioned to several people that Oleta and I would soon be retiring and leaving Greensburg. No one has been ever so warmly received by a group of people like Oleta and I were received by the Russell Creek Association. Our rapport had been such that no one could utter a negative word about us.

Oleta and I have always wanted to do exactly what God wants us to do. That's why we were on the move. Our Father in Heaven just said, "Your time is finished here, so follow me." Like Abraham of Old, we were striking out again and following His directions. Our life is His, so whatever opens up, we want to be there.

When I announced to both of the Associations that my final day as Director of Missions and Oleta's as the Associational Secretary would be December 31, 1992, it came as a shock. This had been one of our best years in many ways. The youth were reaching a record number in their work. The WMU was blossoming out in a new direction. Men who were once timid were now boldly carrying on for God. Every church in both Associations had a pastor right now. The Association has a good name, and is firmly established. Indeed, my work there was finished. We said, "God bless you, and thank you for your love and care." to everyone we could before we left.

Even though my duties as Director of Missions had ended, we were not ready to move away just yet.

Chapter 27

Retirement—Yet Lots To Do

It was Monday January 4, 1993, in Greensburg, as I strolled up the street of that little town, our home since July of 1980, to pay some utility bills. Some people I met heard that we were leaving Greensburg and moving to Florida. I finally reached the Dairy Queen, at 220 South Main Street, where I was to meet Reverend Ancil Durrett, one of my good pastor friends, for a cup of coffee. As I went over to be seated by Reverend Durrett, several people asked me why I was leaving Greensburg. One man said rather boldly, "I hope you like it down there in that sand with the ants."

After my meeting with Reverend Durrett, I returned to my home. Since Oleta was at work, at the Green County Health Department, I was all alone! No job! And not a person I met encouraged Oleta and me one little bit to move to Florida. I thought, as I walked through the house from room to room and ending up in my office, this was the room I had remodeled in 1980 just for the Associational office. This was the room that had the bookcases that my father and I had built together. At the very back was that big work bench and it was now loaded with new equipment that the Association had purchased.

I went over and sat down at that desk that the automobile dealer in London bought and donated for this office. I opened the file cabinet and looked at it, now filled with the results of events held in the Association. I stopped right there and thanked God for this automobile dealer, who loved God enough to help this struggling boy from Back Creek to open this office. As I sat down in that chair, the office was quiet and little tears came to my eyes.

Was I all alone? No, Almighty God was by my side watching my every move. Yet in that office, I found myself thinking did I know what I was doing? Why did I work so hard to accomplish these breakthroughs, only to walk away? Suddenly, these words came to my mind, "Remember the fall of 1951 at Georgetown College, when you got that letter from the college Dean telling you that you were about to flunk out of college?"

Then I remembered what the Lord said to me, "If you will take care of My business, I will take care of you." I didn't have to listen to what these people were saying. Almighty God took care of his servants Elijah and Elisha. Didn't He also take care of Paul at Ephesus where he did the most marvelous works during his ministry. Multitudes of Diana worshipers became Christians and churches were formed in cities for a hundred miles around. I should do what God is calling me to do and He will take care of me.

Oleta came in from work that night and as we were eating dinner at our little kitchen table I said, "We are going to move to Florida."

She immediately said, "When are we going to make the move?"

Chapter 27 — Retirement—Yet Lots To Do

I told her I didn't really know when we were going to move, but we were going to move. Before she could respond, I said, "God may have more work around here for me to do yet. Remember He is in control. We just have to have faith."

Oleta and I sat there at the table that night, just like we sat out in front of her house at 531 Pelham Street, and I talked to her and told her God was calling me to Pike County to start a church in a pioneer field where there were no Baptist churches. I told her I remembered it was the week of January 28, 1957, and I had been there looking over this vast mission field when I dropped a two cent postcard in the mail to her. I quickly wrote to tell her this would be our future field of work. I said, "It will probably be slow but God wants our best."

When I left Oleta that week in January 1957, I never saw her again until she came, with her sister and mother, to Williamson, West Virginia, the first week in June 1957. We made it then and we will make it now. We got married and here we are now. Then I told her Mark Twain once said something like this, "Life is just one darn thing after another." That's just the way life is in this imperfect world. The Bible teaches us that the blood of Jesus Christ does not cover your sins, cancel your sins, postpone your sins, or diminish your sins. It takes away your sins, once and for all time.

We continued to talk about those twelve disciples in the book of Acts. They had all received the Baptism of the Holy Spirit at Pentecost, and the Church was born. But it wasn't long until James was killed, and Peter and John were put in jail for preaching about Jesus. What I am trying to say, is that there is no stability in this imperfect world. So I reasoned, "Where do we find stability in this topsy-turvy world? It is found only by anchoring our Faith on the unchanging, everlasting Lord whose promises never, never fail." (See Deuteronomy 33:27 and 4:31, Isaiah 41:17, and Hebrews 12:5).

I told Oleta, "Our joy and hope can be steady as the sun rises, even when we hear derogatory remarks on the work we dedicated to God. This Bible teaches that God does not lie and that His Promises hold today." (See Titus 1:2, Hebrews 6:18, and Psalm 105:42).

Having faith in God and His word can be a fairly straightforward thing. It requires His followers to depend on Almighty God to keep His Promises.

Oleta and I have been on Mission for Christ and have never, never been disappointed. God is true to His word. He keeps the promises that He makes to His Children. (See 2 Peter 1:4, Psalm 105:42, Romans 4:20, and Timothy 4:8).

When I returned from that Evangelistic Mission in Russia, Oleta had just about completed the sale of our Greensburg property. God was keeping His promise to those who walk by faith.

God had said to me in January, "I still have some work for you to do." God did it and He provided for it in a remarkable way. All by faith. Almighty God, began his journey with us when He left His throne in Heaven and came as a little baby at

Chapter 27 — Retirement—Yet Lots To Do

Bethlehem. Armed with nothing more than a passion to win your heart, He came looking. The Bible has a word for this quest called reconciliation. (See 2 Corinthians 5:19–21).

Oleta and I closed the selling of the house in Greensburg and were able to load up our furnishings and move out on August 23, 1993. We left Kentucky but Kentucky did not leave us. We drove by Glasgow and Scottsville in Kentucky, and then we went by Lebanon and Murfreesboro in Tennessee where we got on Route 24 east toward Chattanooga, Tennessee, From there we got on Interstate 75 South toward Atlanta, Georgia and Orlando, Florida. We got as far as Jennings, Florida, where we spent the night at a Scottish Inn hotel. The next day we drove the rest of the way to our new home at 12227 Wedgefield Drive, Leesburg, Florida.

We soon started unloading our vehicles. A neighbor across the street saw us unloading and came across and helped us with the heavy items. We took the rental truck and trailer back to a U–Haul dealer at Leesburg, Florida. It is interesting how our Lord does His mighty work. God is full of wonders. (See Joshua 3:5, Psalm 77:14, Acts 2:43, and Revelation 13:13).

Oleta and I had bought a lot to build a house in Palm Beach County, Florida, several years earlier because her sister, Colleen, and her husband, Jim Ramsey, lived in Palm Beach County.

In 1989, our son, Lyndon, decided to leave the Commonwealth of Kentucky Department of Transportation and migrate to Florida with the idea of finding better work. He found an apartment in the Leesburg area and after working at several different jobs, landed a job with the United Telephone Company of Florida in Altamonte Springs in September 1989. It looked as if it would be a good permanent job. Oleta and I visited him in the fall of 1990 at his apartment. He sent us the directions to where he was staying and we drove right up to his apartment. It was small but good enough for a single young man.

We stayed with him several days. We went out sight seeing in the day time and came back at night when he was home from work. The floor was our bed, but we threw down the sheets and cover, and with pillows, we made it just fine. I told Oleta we could purchase a lot here in Lake County and build a house for Lyndon to live in until we retired.

Late one day as were driving back from Orlando, the sun was setting in the western Florida sky and suddenly we saw a sign on the side of the road, "Lots for Sale." It was on County Road 44, not far from where Lyndon was living. We arrived at the sales office for the Wedgewood development project just about closing time. The kind and gracious gentleman took us out and showed us Lot 52 and I felt this would be a great place to build a house.

I walked out in the weeds, some were up to my waist, and it seemed like God said, "This is it." So I said to Oleta we should make a deal right here. We quickly went back to the office where we closed the deal as quickly as Moses got his instructions in the desert to go back to Egypt.

Chapter 27 — Retirement—Yet Lots To Do

The gentleman said we would need to pick out the kind of house we wanted on the lot. He quickly showed us several building plans and advised us to take them back to Kentucky so we could decide which one we liked.

Oleta and I got back in the car shaken up and starry eyed. As we drove away I remarked, "That's the quickest I believe I ever made a big deal like that."

My dear Oleta said, "We will have to borrow the money to get this house paid for."

I reminded her that the Bible says in Psalm 95:7, "For he is our God; and we are the people of his pasture, and the sheep of his hand." Then she said to me, with that keen look in her eyes, teaching me like a seminary Bible professor with some quick words from the Psalm 84:11, "...no good thing will he withhold from them that walk uprightly." The children of Israel didn't understand a lot of things as Moses led them out in the desert. The Bible says in Psalm 62:8, "Trust in him at all times; ye people, pour out your heart before him: God is a refuge for us." I told Oleta that I firmly believe we made the correct decision, and we would get rid of that lot in Palm Beach County.

When we got to Lyndon's apartment, he had just come in and we told him what had happened. He was excited! He said he would watch as the house was being constructed and he would take pictures to send to us.

Oleta and I left Florida the next day and headed for Greensburg, Kentucky. On the way home, I said to Oleta not to tell anyone about the deal. If it doesn't work, we were sunk. If it does go over, we may be here in Florida when I retire.

In early 1991, we had to make several trips to Florida to see the construction of the house and sign papers for a loan to pay for the house and lot.

That Girl from 531 Pelham Street said to me, "When you decide on something it sure is quick."

With a twinkle in my eye, I chuckled, "Remember that's the way I got you."

She agreed it was quick and reminded me she both wrote to me and prayed for me. I told her that I remember getting those letters and they sure kept me fired up.

I said, "I guess I do act quick sometimes. I remember in a letter you wrote on May 1, 1957, you said, 'I still don't know all about you, do I?'"

That is the way it is with the boy from Back Creek. When I feel like God is telling me to do something, I just jump right out and do it. That's what the Bible teaches. Remember Luke 6:46 NIV, "Why do you call me, 'Lord, Lord,' and do not do what I say?" That's where my faith comes in. I believe my God honors people who will jump out and follow Almighty God's word.

God told me, while I was out there riding my pony, to go to Georgetown College. I just struck out and went. I didn't

Chapter 27 — Retirement—Yet Lots To Do

understand much about it. I just jumped up and followed God's leadership. God told me to ask Oleta to marry me. I didn't have to know it all, it was just what God asked me to do. I believe Oleta and I were called to press on, to press on even if we didn't understand it all. With Jesus in the navigator's seat of our journey through life, we can press on to the finish line.

When the house was finished Oleta and I went to Florida and signed all the proper papers. The house and lot were deeded to us. At once we let Lyndon move into the house and he was well pleased and we felt comfortable, that he was there taking good care of everything. Due to the housing growth in that area, our address had changed from 12227 Wedgefield Drive, Leesburg, Florida, to 12227 Wedgefield Drive, Grand Island, Florida.

In October of 1991 Lyndon ruptured a disc in the lower back and was operated on in Orlando. Oleta and I immediately went to Florida to see him. Oleta put her job at the health department on hold and decided to stay at our new house with him until he recovered. With a lot of prayer he made a near-full recovery and Oleta was able to return to Kentucky in March of 1992.

When Oleta and I arrived in Florida in 1993, we noticed that the Grand Island Baptist Church was preparing to meet in their new building on September 19, 1993. We were there the first Sunday in the new building. Oleta and I quickly moved our Church Membership to Grand Island Baptist Church, where we attended many Associational events in the Lake County Baptist Association.

My past experience was quickly utilized as a supply pastor. I enjoyed every minute of it. Therefore, I offered these services to the Florida Baptist Convention at 1230 Hendricks Avenue, Jacksonville, Florida 32207.

My work as a supply minister in Baptist churches sometimes lasted quite awhile and it was a helpful and wonderful Ministry. Some of the churches I assisted were: Paisley, Mineola, Altoona, Mascotte, Groveland, Okahumpka, Pine Lakes, Astatula, Umatilla, Lake Ola, Sarrento, and Central Baptist and Mid–way Baptist in Leesburg.

I also wrote to the American Bible Society at 1865 Broadway, New York, New York 10023 and asked them if they had any volunteer Ministry in Florida. Dr. Haveland C. Houston, Director of Volunteer Activities/Field Services, wrote back and said at this time she was not aware of any openings in Florida.

However, in a few weeks she notified me that Reverend John Vanderbeck, who lived in Florida, was resigning as Florida State Coordinator and that he would call and discuss the work with me and perhaps I could take his place.

It was not long until Dr. John Vanderbeck and his wife met with Oleta and me at a restaurant in Leesburg for lunch. We discussed the work of the American Bible Society and how it functioned in Ministry in Florida. Dr. Vanderbeck agreed to

Chapter 27 — Retirement—Yet Lots To Do

turn all his responsibility with the American Bible Society in Florida over to me at once. Dr. Haveland C. Houston wrote to invite me to New York in October 1994 for a special meeting. I went and was thoroughly pleased with what I saw and felt at the meeting.

The next time I went to New York for a meeting with the American Bible Society, Oleta attended with me. We were officially recognized as the Florida State Coordinators for the American Bible Society.

In 1995 the American Bible Society came out with the First Edition of the Contemporary English Version of the Holy Bible. I was appointed as an ambassador on November 4, 1995 and helped launch the Contemporary English Version of the Bible.

Oleta and I did a great deal of traveling in the State of Florida, visiting volunteers, and recruiting volunteers to help distribute God's Word. We labored in Tampa, Lakeland, Miami, Jacksonville, Tallahassee, Daytona Beach, Melbourne, Orlando, Winter Haven, Winter Park, Apopka and many other cities working with groups of people who wanted to see God's Word put in the hands of more people in Florida.

In 1996 Oleta and I were in a training session at the American Bible Society headquarters at 1865 Broadway, New York, New York, where I took training to be a National Speaker. I often spoke at churches, conventions, clubs, and organizations about the Ministry and work of the American Bible Society.

One of the most interesting ministries was representing the American Bible Society at religious conventions across the state of Florida. When some denominations met in Florida they often wanted to hear from the work of the American Bible Society and I would put up a large display of Bibles and materials that the American Bible Society published. I was present to answer questions and explain the Ministry of the American Bible Society. Our American genius for solutions that provide order and at the same time win people to Jesus Christ was what thrilled people.

Because the headquarters of the American Bible Society was in New York City, Oleta and I had the opportunity to visit the Twin Towers, the Empire State Building and several other famous sites there.

Dr. Faye Flemister became the director of the Volunteer Department after Dr. Haveland C. Houston retired, and remained in that position until changes were made in the Ministry.

Oleta and I really did enjoy those years as co-laborers with the American Bible Society. It takes a lot of faith to be a volunteer in the Master's Ministry. There is nothing the Lord wants of us more than the exercise of our faith. He will do nothing to undermine it, and we cannot please Him without it. What is faith? It is believing that which has no absolute proof. (See Hebrews 11:1). It is hanging tough when the evidence would have you bail out. It is determining to trust God when

Chapter 27 — Retirement—Yet Lots To Do

He has not answered all our questions or even assured a pain-free passage.

Quick to learn and always eager to pitch in, Oleta stood tall with those at every level of the American Bible Society. She was undaunted even by those at the New York City main office. Oleta took full charge of the Literacy with the American Bible Society and made it her mission to visit the local American Bible Society office in Jerusalem, Israel. It takes people with faith who will rise up and do their best reclaiming their streets and neighborhoods and are optimistic about the future.

I remember, on one of our visits in New York City, as Oleta and I looked out the window of our hotel room, we could see the people wandering around in Central Park. It reminded us that God gave Abraham some very important information, but He did not give him a road map. Why did God do this? He wanted Abraham and Sarah to just trust Him for the journey. I said to my dearest, "I was just thinking about the time I held your hand and put that ring on your finger. I didn't know where we were headed, but look where we are right now." Abraham did not know where they were headed, but he knew their future would be blessed by Almighty God. Back then we did not know we would ever be here in the Big Apple, but we let our God hold the traveling plans and here we are. It's not anything either of us has done, but what God has done.

Oleta whispered in a quiet calm voice, "Jim it's all by Faith. Life is so much better when you follow God's plan." We prayed together before we left the hotel and went to the American Bible Society building. This was how our years were spent with the American Bible Society—going places, talking with people, selling Bibles, and giving away Bibles and New Testaments to needy people. Just by faith we were getting out the Word of God to a hungry and desperate world.

We watched the joy come to boys' and girls' lives as they, for the first time in life on planet Earth, were able to have a Bible they could read and call their own. The Contemporary English Version of God's word just lights up the lives of many people, because it makes the Word of God easy to understand.

This thing of faith is so wonderful that only Almighty God could put a girl from 531 Pelham Street and a boy from Back Creek together for the journey of life and be here in New York City. As Oleta and I were being entertained one night in a restaurant on Broadway, I whispered in her ear, "This is a big jump from that mush my mother fixed for our family at night during the great depression days."

Oleta smiled and said, "It sure is better than the cracklings we had at our house."

On May 26, 2000, the American Bible Society had a recognition banquet at 1865 Broadway, New York, New York, for all the volunteers, who by faith, had so wonderfully given of their time and talents to this great cause of distributing God's word without fear and trembling here in the United States of America.

Chapter 27 — Retirement—Yet Lots To Do

When Oleta and I decided to move to Florida, we did not know what was really ahead of us. We were simply following the leadership of God's Holy Spirit. As far as we could see with our human eyes and feel with our human hands, we had no real direction about our future here on earth. As blood-bought children of Almighty God, we stayed close to Jesus. We had a habit of staying close to God and we knew that was the main thing to do.

Because Oleta and I were around Christian people and made ourselves available, we saw the miracle growth of the Grand Island Baptist Church. Reverend David Williams was called as the first full-time pastor and under his leadership I served and assisted in teaching the Bible as the Lord opened up opportunities. Oleta soon found her place in the WMU and working with the children in Sunday School. The Bible says in Romans 8:28, "All things work together for good to them that love God." Yes, God was at work in Lake County, Florida. The Lord soon opened up opportunities for the boy from Back Creek to preach in several Baptist Churches across the Lake County Baptist Association.

During the time we lived in Florida, I was interim pastor at the following churches : Central Baptist Church, Leesburg; Lake Ola Baptist Church, Tangerine; First Baptist Church, Sorrento; and Mid-Way Baptist Church, Leesburg. In every Church, there were additions to the Church membership and the Churches were all revived and doing the work of evangelism and ministering to the needs of people in the community. Remember the second half of Romans 8:28 it says that God brings about "good to them that love God." Oleta and I don't always understand every little thing our God is doing, but we sure do love God in Heaven with all our heart, soul and might. (See Deuteronomy 6:5 and Matthew 22:37). Our God doesn't ask us to understand Him, but to simply LOVE HIM.

We aren't asked today to have our hands nailed to a cross. We aren't asked to be spit upon or wear a crown of thorns. But we are asked to love God with all our heart. That's why I preach about the "Horrors of Hell." Our God did not keep back His own Son, but He gave Him for us. If God did this, won't He freely give us everything else? (See Romans 8:32). Some of you who are reading this right now, perhaps are saying, "will this 'Faith' really work." Let me suggest to you, leave all your bad moments, your mad moments, and your anxious moments at the foot of the Cross. Unless Jesus Christ comes first, you will have one final moment, a final breath, a final beating of the heart and in a split second you will leave this world you now know and enter what you have never seen.

Chapter 28
My Aging Mother And Father

While Oleta and I were living at Greensburg, I would often stop by the home of my mother and father in Mount Eden when I was going to a meeting in Louisville or Lexington. I noticed as I stopped by there early in 1986 that my mother was not feeling well and there seemed to be a slight memory problem. I watched as my father tried to correct her on certain issues. I discussed this with Oleta and we supposed my mother could be in the early stages of that dreaded Alzheimer's disease.

A couple of years later, my father was doing some work on a neighboring building and he fell from a ladder. He was taken to the hospital in Shelbyville, but was soon released. A few months went by and he seemed alright. Suddenly, he passed out and was taken to the same hospital. His doctor put him on some medicine. Then one day, he and my mother went to Shelbyville to get some groceries. While he was stopped at a traffic light, he suddenly passed out and the car ran across the street into an electrical pole. He again was taken to the hospital and his doctor gave him an intensive physical exam. The doctor advised him to quit driving. Not very long afterwards my father sold his automobile. He looked to his family to help with getting to the medical doctors and getting groceries.

Since Oleta and I had moved to Florida in August 1993, it made it harder for my father and mother to get the assistance they needed. I came up from Florida several times to assist with things. Jeff and Barry did all they could, but they both had full time jobs and their own families.

Sometime in June 1994, Barry called me and let me know that something must be done because my parents' health problems were worsening. I wrote my father and told him that I would help him find a nice house for them in Florida, but he would have to sell his house in Kentucky first.

He gave me the okay to look for a house, so Lyndon and I began looking around the neighborhoods for a house. Finally, we located one in Mid–Florida Lakes, a mobile home development, just off County Road 44. It was only about three miles from our house. My father consented and we began the process to make the move south.

My father agreed to buy the house in Mid–Florida Lakes, so he put his house and lot in Mount Eden, up for sale. I drove up to Kentucky to help them get things ready for the sale. The sale went very well and my dad was very pleased.

Their new house in Florida was completely furnished so my father sold everything he didn't need. We loaded their belongings in a U–Haul trailer which I pulled behind my car.

On Monday, following the sale on Saturday, we went by Shelbyville and did what was necessary to finalize the sale. Afterwards, my parents and myself headed toward Florida. We could not make the entire trip that day, so we pulled into a motel in Georgia for the night. The next day we arrived at Mid–Florida Lakes, located on the north side of Lake Eustis.

Chapter 28 — My Aging Mother And Father

My parents were very well pleased with their new house. It was newly furnished inside and had a nice car port.

Shortly after getting settled in the community, my father bought himself a new three-wheel bike to ride up to the club house or to the lake. However, he thought it would be better for both of them if they had a golf cart to ride around in the park. They could drive to the club house and the lake to do some fishing. He sold the three-wheel bike and bought a golf cart. He kept the golf cart until just before he decided to leave his house in Mid-Florida Lakes.

I took my mother and father to see many of the attractions in Central Florida. They both had a lot of fun and really enjoyed Florida. For several years we purchased senior tickets for the Silver Springs attraction at Ocala. We went there often and rode in the glass-bottom boats and enjoyed the attractions at the park.

Eventually my mother became very ill and was hospitalized at the Leesburg Regional Medical Center. Later she was transferred to a local nursing home.

She returned home briefly, but her health continued to deteriorate. She returned to the local nursing home in the Fall of 1997. My mother passed away on November 11, 1997. She was brought back to Shelbyville, Kentucky, for funeral services and burial. She was buried at Grove Hill Cemetery in Shelbyville, on November 14, 1997.

My father continued to live in Mid–Florida Lakes until September 2004. As a result of the three hurricanes of 2004, Charley, Frances, and Jeanne, that devastated central Florida, my father decided to move in with my son, Lyndon, and his family. They had a vacant room available. Lyndon only lived two houses from where Oleta and I lived, in the Wedgwood subdivision.

My daughter, Sibyl, and her husband, Don Stricklin, had bought additional property in Kentucky that joined theirs and wanted Oleta and me to buy a lot from them. We could then build a house and move back to Kentucky. In 2006, Oleta and I did purchase the lot that faced Moore Road in Williamsburg. The lot previously had a house on it, but had been torn down. On September 15, 2006, the contractor started on our new house. Oleta put on her decorator's hat and worked with Sears at Corbin to get appliances and accessories for our new Kentucky home.

Our Florida house was listed with Jim Williams of Century 21. He was able sell our house, so we were able to move out on March 14, 2007. I drove a loaded Penske truck and pulled a U–Haul trailer behind it. Oleta followed in our Buick car with my father at her side. We happily arrived at our new home in Williamsburg, Kentucky, on March 15, 2007.

Chapter 29

Closing Years

Our testimony did not stop in Florida; it continued until our leader, the Lord Jesus Christ, returned us to Kentucky. With a refreshed faith in God, Oleta, my father, and myself, re-settled in the beloved hills of Kentucky. Oleta and I talked about how we would like to help some small Baptist church down in a valley or nestled in a hollow. However, these dreams were soon smashed as my father was the first one of the three of us in the household to hear the death call start rattling.

However, before he met his Maker, Oleta fell victim to cancer. She had fought that monster before and the medical professionals had announced she was clear of that giant monster. Like a tiger waiting to catch its meal, cancer sprung up in the liver and pancreas this time and it was battling for her very life. Oleta marched right into it, confident it would be defeated. The skilled hands of doctors and nurses came to her side and entered the battle with her. I remember one nurse looking me in the eye and saying, "She has the faith of David when he faced Goliath the giant." (See 1 Samuel 17). Goliath was nine feet tall, his armor weighed one hundred fifty pounds, and his spear head about twenty pounds. David faced him with a staff and a sling with five smooth stones he picked up out of the creek. David got the victory because he trusted his God. This victory thrilled his people.

Oleta had been thrilling people from New York to Florida and in every state she marched into serving with the American Bible Society because of her faith in Almighty God. But there comes a time when God's great warriors must give in to death. As her husband and life partner, I did not want to see her pass from my side, but I longed to encourage her. I read to her from Hebrews 9:27, "It is appointed unto men once to die." I reminded her that at a Christian's death, he or she is at once "With the Lord" and this body awaits resurrection at the return of Jesus Christ. (See 2 Corinthians 5:1–8).

One day in August 2011, my wise and understanding wife came into my little humble office room, in the corner of our bedroom, and sat down in the big chair across from me and said, "Jim, I don't think this body of mine is going to throw off this sickness." Little tears came in her eyes as she tried to smile in my presence, then she quietly got up and left the room.

On September 4, 2011, Oleta and I observed our birthdays together for the last time on planet Earth. Oleta was seventy-seven and I was eighty-one. Oh, what a journey it had been since I saw her in September 1956 at her twenty-second birthday gathering. That was the first time I ever kissed her but it wasn't the last. It seemed that after all the children and grand children had gone to their homes, Oleta and I were left alone to spend our last months together, closer than perhaps before in all our fifty-four years of marriage.

It was obvious that the cancer was eating its way to the very heart of Oleta's life. On Monday, November 7, 2011, at

Chapter 29 — Closing Years

about bed time, Oleta said, "I believe I will come in there and sleep with you tonight." I knew she loved me and wanted these last hours by my side.

I said, "That's good, but I have a doctor's appointment in the morning at 8:00 a.m. in Corbin." She came in the bedroom and slept by the one she had pledged to be with "till death do we part."

On Wednesday, November 9, 2011, at 9:15 a.m., I had another doctor's appointment in London and for the second time in a week I left her alone in the house.

When Thursday, November 10, 2011, dawned, there was evidence in Oleta's body that she was facing life's last battle. I called all the children and family members to come home at once. It appeared that their mother would soon be passing from Earth to be with Jesus forever.

On Saturday, November 12, 2011, Oleta made a turn toward that final end, as she fought against that terrible pain from head to toe in her body. By Sunday morning, November 13, 2011 Oleta lay almost senseless and motionless, on one side, her head on a pillow and her eyes closed. At about 2:00 a.m. Monday morning, November 14, 2011, I was suddenly awakened and arose; she had breathed her last breath. The boy from Back Creek was all chocked up because this was the toughest thing he had ever faced in life. However, within minutes all four of our children were at my side. It's great when you have to walk through times like this, you don't have to do it alone. My God was right there as He had promised. (See Deuteronomy 33:27 and Psalm 84:11).

The Croley Funeral Home at 102 South Second Street, Williamsburg, was in charge of the funeral arrangements. The Funeral was conducted on November 17, 2011 at the Croley Funeral Home Chapel. Reverend Bill Wright, brought the message and Dr. Jeff Smoak sung two songs, "I'd Rather Have Jesus" and "The Longer I Serve Him the Sweeter He Grows."

Oleta was buried in the Mason County Cemetery, Maysville, Kentucky on November 17, 2011.

The Girl from 531 Pelham Street, Maysville, Kentucky, had completed her earthly mission. She left the pain ridden, worn out body. Doing the will of her Father in Heaven, and joined by her friends, she entered the celestial city whose builder and maker is God.

I reached into that casket and placed a kiss on her like the boy from Back Creek had so often done in life. I thanked Almighty God for the joy she brought to my life and the lives of so many more across the country—for she lived to share her life with the world.

Scores of people came and marched by that casket to pay their respects to her for such a faithful life. In the crowd were several students to whom she had taught God's word in Vacation Bible School and Sunday School. Messages and flowers came from so many places across the nation.

Chapter 29 — Closing Years

We learned many lessons in faith as we faced the constant challenge of enjoying each other and our growing family because we always had a limited income. There were several months when the Lord provided a miracle in our behalf so we could make it. The Bible meant much to us. We read from it everyday. This was where we drew our strength. (See Psalm 91:11–12, Psalm 92:12–15, Psalm 37:7, Psalm 119:105, Philippians 4:13, and Revelation 3:20). Our ministry together started in 1957. We have served on the cutting edge of life. We have never rattled a tin cup or begged for support. We have depended upon Almighty God and the prayers of God's faithful children, and we were never disappointed.

I remember one night, after being critically ill for several months, Oleta was sleeping in a hospital bed in the second bedroom on the other end of the house from where I was sleeping. Suddenly, Almighty God shook me from my slumber and a voice said, "Look, look." I sat up in my bed and watched Oleta riding in a chariot up toward Heaven. It lifted her up and up—toward Heaven. The driver of the chariot was the one she had taken as her personal savior at age twelve. Yes, He was the one who was at her side the night that I asked her to be my wife. He was the one who presided over our wedding on June 22, 1957. He was the one who was letting me see how she would go to glory. I sat there in my bed and watched, because her Lord and Master wanted me to see the final end. Yes, I got to see it because God had brought us together for a little more than fifty-four years and He had promised me that if I would do His will that He would take care of me. (See Matthew 6:33 and John 14:13–14).

If you want to know about how committed God is to take care of His people read, Genesis 18:14, Psalm 18:30, and Psalm 37:4.

God will keep His promise to us. Remember what happened to Jacob? Read about Jacob in Genesis 28:10–22. Now and then God has to come to us today in strange ways to keep His promise to us.

One summer night in June of 2012, soon after going to bed, I suddenly heard soft music playing and someone singing. I got out of bed to see what it was and to my right just a few feet away I saw Oleta sitting in a chair dressed in a beautiful, flowery dress. She was looking straight at me but did not say a word. As I moved a little closer to her she faded away. Then I heard a voice say, "The next time you see her you will be at her side." What God promises He will do.

Chapter 30
In The Middle Of A Storm

We had a lot of storms hit Back Creek where I grew up in Shelby County, Kentucky. They would hit quick and swift. The creek would rise out of its banks and flood our front yard. These storms did damage to our crops, our gardens, and sometimes killed people. They came when you weren't expecting them.

In Florida, we lived northwest of Orlando and felt fairly secure from the hurricanes. However, in 2004, we were right in the paths of three that came barreling down on us. It is difficult to know what to do in the midst of a terrible, frightening storm. We huddled down and watched out our windows as our neighbor's roof blew away.

There are storms that come into our lives all the time. Perhaps you have faced a tragedy in your family and wondered how to handle it. Looking back I think about the time we found out that our son Jeffrey had a learning disability called dyslexia. I am not sure when we first heard the thunder rumbling. We had to deal with it and there was a price our family had to bear.

In 1977 my mother and father observed their fiftieth wedding anniversary at the Mount Moriah Baptist Church fellowship hall in Mount Eden, Kentucky. It was beautiful and wonderful in every way. However, in 1986 my father began to notice that there were changes coming along in my mother's life and he did not understand what he should do. I told him that I thought it was the beginning of Alzheimer's disease. Then I proceeded to tell him about this disease. It grew worse each year and when they observed their sixtieth wedding anniversary at their house in 1987, she did not have the same excitement or understanding about it as she had at the fiftieth wedding anniversary.

In 1994 I had my mother and father sell their home and buy a comfortable house in Florida near Oleta and me so we could meet their needs. They seemed to enjoy the climate and the beauty of Florida but my mother's condition continued to worsen. She had trouble swallowing food and at times didn't even want to eat. Her expressions changed and there seemed to be less joy in life. Someone who had always been full of fun and joy, was now almost silent. Finally we had to take her to a nursing home where she soon slipped away to be with Jesus forever on November 11, 1997.

My Father was always a brave person and the family leader. But the storm hit him and caused him to reel and rock back and forth. He fought a gallant battle but at the age of 102 on October 22, 2009, he went home to be with the Lord he had served and loved with all his heart.

When Oleta was first told she had breast cancer in 1985, it was like a rolling thunder in our family. We had been telling people that this earth is not our home; we're just strangers here for a brief visit while we are seeking the City that is to come.

Chapter 30 — In The Middle Of A Storm

She had the risky operation and the surgeon said he got all the cancer. Years passed and she was declared clean of this monster. It's hard to understand all the cost of a raving storm in your life. (See I Peter 4:1–19, 2 Timothy 3:12, 1 Peter 5:10, 2 Timothy 2:3, James 4:14, and Hebrews 9:22).

When the second storm of cancer struck Oleta in 2009, it was real and devastating. It ate its way day by day and those who were close to her could see the monsters at work. Like a mighty hurricane, the cancer swept through her body. Finally, she said good–bye to this world and entered that land of rest with her Lord and Master, Jesus Christ.

During Oleta's sickness, I had my own storm coming ashore in my life. In 1993 I had a hiatal hernia operation; in January 2009 lower back operation; in June 2009 gall bladder operation; in November 2010 kidney stone operation; and in January 2011 hernia operation. If that was not enough, the tornado of a tumor on the brain was finally made known. The rattling of these things can make you nervous. What do you do when the winds blow and blow and don't seem to settle down? Here is what God told me, "Get it in writing right now about your life so others can profit by reading your story." That's exactly what the boy from Back Creek is doing as you read this book. Some of the people who read this book are right now trying to figure out why things are like they are in their life. I know people don't read books that don't interest them in some way. I say this honestly, I hope that as you read the pages of this book, you will find relief, wisdom, and comfort as you live on planet earth. Friend, don't go through the hard times and just say, "Well this is just a part of life." My God wants to accomplish something in your life, in your home, in your business, or in the life of someone in your household. Almighty God's word is true. Almighty God keeps his promise. When a storm hits your life, don't give up, don't fuss, and don't blame others. A human being doesn't have what it takes to get through the storms along life's path, but, my God has it all. (See Psalm 50:10, Psalm 34:17–19, Psalm 37:16, Proverbs 22:1, Psalm 119:105, Psalm 119:112, Psalm 119:160, and Job 23:10). If it was left up to us, we would hide or dodge all these storms, but these storms prepare us for that place called Heaven.

Chapter 31
The Call To Obey

The word I heard my mother and father use a lot around the house and on the farm down on Back Creek was obey. My mother and father expected me to obey them. If I did not, there was some kind of punishment on the way. In the public school system there were specific rules to follow or we would be punished. It is the same way in God's world. (See Psalm 111:10 and Numbers 32:23). If a person doesn't obey Almighty God, trouble is on its way. Someone said one day, "This boy from Back Creek sure has a lot of faith. To hear him talk, God is bigger than all the creeds and isms in this world." That girl from 531 Pelham Street said, "There is no one else like Jim. He believes in serving Jesus and Him only."

On that farm in Kentucky with my parents, I had a desire to do right. That was one reason I was slow to accept God's call on my life to be a preacher of the Word of God. I wrestled with God's call for three years, before I was willing by faith to go with God's plan for my life. I would often go into the woods and kneel down and pray for hours, battling this idea of being God's Preacher Man. Sometimes I would wander across the hillside and down to the creek that flowed by the farm, crying and weeping and struggling to know the real will of God for my life. I would often stay up late at night reading the Bible, trying to search for God's will in that blessed Holy Bible. I read of Gideon's struggle with God in Judges chapters six and seven where he asked God to make clear to him what he was supposed to do. Riding my pony sometimes I would find myself crying and pleading with God about how could I be a Preacher Man for Him. I did not want to make a mistake. Finally, after more than three years, trying to figure it all out, I realized I must jump out on faith and simply take God at His word.

That's exactly what I did on June 10, 1951. I stepped out on faith in front of everybody in the Mount Moriah Baptist Church in Mount Eden, Kentucky and told them God had called me to preach His word. When I took God at His Word, even though I did not have a road map for my life, it began to open up one step at a time. I said to my home church and to the world, if Abraham could walk by faith out of a heathen environment, I could walk by faith in this world. That's what I did and I never turned back. My call was so real and ablaze in my heart that I was not content unless I was active in the preaching ministry.

At Georgetown College I was anxious to help start a new Mission Church. I was glad to stand on the street corner and preach God's Word. It thrilled me to preach in the local jail, to visit the local hospital, and to tell people about John 3:16. (See Jeremiah 20:9, Amos 4:11, Philippians 1:21, and 1 Corinthians 9:19). I was thrust out by a mighty force of the Holy Spirit at age twenty. I knew there was a big world out there and I wanted to get into it with all I had. At age twenty-four, I was called of God to Missionary work at McRoberts Baptist Church, McRoberts, Kentucky. I went out with the everlasting

Chapter 31 — The Call To Obey

Gospel on my mind day and night. I was up hollows and crossing foot bridges telling people about John 3:16. I knelt down in my little mountain cottage and pleaded with God for souls. In two years time God gave forty-eight new members to the membership roll of the McRoberts Baptist Church. In December of 1955 I was called upon by the Home Mission Board of the Southern Baptist Convention to deliver the message of Jesus in a Mission Conference in Blytheville, Arkansas. Little did I think at that time, that would be the beginning of a life time Mission with the Home Mission Board in going to different places, telling the story of Redemption and God's love in fifteen states in the United States of America.

I remember Oleta and I went to watch our daughter, Sibyl Stricklin, run in a race in Williamsburg. While standing there, I rubbed up against a light post on the side of the side walk and got a little injury on my left arm. It wasn't bad and soon got well. While talking, as we waited for Sibyl to come across the finish line, I said to Oleta, "I have always had bumps in my life and I guess, they keep me close to Jesus." Just like the Apostle Paul had a thorn in the flesh according to II Corinthians 12:7, and it kept him close to God all his life. Right there on the street corner I talked about when I was three and four years old, I was a stutterer, some words I couldn't speak plainly. I recalled when I was about ten years old, it was discovered I had a twisted back and I wore a back brace for about two years, and when I was fourteen and fifteen years old, I developed severe headaches. I remembered when we lived in Wheelwright, I had a bad case of stomach trouble and Dr.

Patterson sent me to the Pikeville Hospital. I had stomach problems again when we lived in Charlestown and Dr. Goodman sent me to the hospital in Jeffersonville for treatment. I guess the thorn in the flesh was there for a purpose and I used Romans 8:28 to back it up.

Oleta said, "The thorn in your life has made you keep depending on God day by day." I have learned when the times are the toughest, Almighty God is right there to be with me as He promised. Sometimes God allows hard times in our lives, but look at the good that comes from it. God displays His power through our weakness and the people around us are drawn to God in spite of our weakness.

Now, I have never enjoyed the thorn or really liked it. I just submit to it. I am living my life with the thorn no matter how hard the personal attacks, insults, failure to speak to me, or a dozen other things come my way. I just keep on doing the main thing—loving people and loving Jesus, because it's His cause I am living for anyway and He said, "My grace is sufficient for thee" (2 Corinthians 12:9).

During most of my ministry there has been the thorn, but I try to be content with the thorn. I want to say right here my wife, the girl from 531 Pelham Street, except for my salvation through Jesus Christ, was God's greatest gift to me. She has walked with me, she has guided me, she has been my partner, she has prayed for me, and she has loved me in spite of my thorns. She has done what I could not do and she has stood by me day and night. She has been with me in the hard times and

Chapter 31 — The Call To Obey

in the good times. She has been God's best gift to me. To God be the Glory! Praise the Lord!

We Christians today need to be like Enoch who walked with God. He laid aside every weight and sin that would keep him from having fellowship with Almighty God. Enoch just sought to be faithful and obedient to Almighty God. The New Testament records Jesus as Saviour twenty–four times and Lord seven hundred and three times. Let's kneel and bow to Him and serve Him. (See Isaiah 41:10).

Chapter 32

The Horrors Of Hell

In my decades of teaching, I realized that many sinners do not consider Jesus seriously because they do not understand the consequences of hell. This factor is imperative and so I am presenting here the essential facts about God's hell. (See Luke 16:19–31).

In Joel 2:1 it says, "Blow ye the trumpet in Zion, and sound an alarm in my holy mountain: let all the inhabitants of the land tremble: for the day of the Lord cometh, for it is nigh at hand." In Amos 5:12 it says, "For I know your manifold transgressions and your mighty sins." And finally in Amos 4:12 it says, "Therefore thus will I do unto thee, O Israel: and because I will do this unto thee, prepare to meet thy God, O Israel."

I ask you today are your prepared to meet Almighty God? If you should die today, would you go to Heaven?

If there was ever a time when we need to preach about hell and seek to win the lost from the flames of hell, it is today. There are more lost people today than there was sixty years ago when I first started preaching in a storefront building in Georgetown, Kentucky.

Religion will not save a person from the flames of hell. Church membership will not save one from the flames of hell. Baptism will not save one from the flames of hell. Being a good moral person will not save one from the flames of hell.

Being a good citizen will not save a person from the flames of hell.

As men in this life have jails, prisons, and penitentiaries in which to put those who break the law, so God in His infinite wisdom must have a prison house for sinners. A prison house for the unsaved dead. The Bible calls this prison house of the dead sinners—HELL! I want us to look at some things about this prison house Almighty God has for sinners.

First, let's look at the certainty of hell. People nowadays serve a weak–kneed, compromising, paper–doll God; one who has all love and mercy, and no justice; one who will wink at sin and let sinners go their way. Modern day teaching is that God has *changed*. But this is not the God of the Bible. The Bible says in Malachi 3:6, "For I am the Lord, I change not."

Revelations 21:8 says, "But the fearful, and unbelieving, and the abominable, and murderers, and whoremongers, and sorcerers, and idolaters, and all liars, shall have their part in the lake which burneth with fire and brimstone, which is the second death." It says in Matthew 10:28, "And fear not them which kill the body, but are not able to kill the soul: but rather fear Him which is able to destroy both soul and body in hell." Furthermore, in Matthew 25:46 it says, "And these shall go away into everlasting punishment: but the righteous into life eternal."

Listen to me very carefully. The same God who rained fire and brimstone on the wicked cities of Sodom and Gomorrah is the same God of today. The God who displayed His wrath

Chapter 32 — The Horrors Of Hell

against sin in the Old Testament by striking men dead with fire, sending plagues, killing the first born children of the Egyptians, drowning Pharaoh and his wicked men in the Red Sea is the same God of today. God will punish sinners. Don't be deceived—there is a hell!

If there is no hell, then this Bible is full of lies. The prophets and apostles are all liars. If there is no hell, this Bible is a myth, a book of fairy tales. The Old Testament speaks about hell, Psalm 9:17 says, "The wicked shall be turned into hell, and all the nations that forget God."

Mark 9:43-44 says, "And if thy hand offend thee, cut it off: it is better for thee to enter into life maimed, than having two hands to go into hell, into the fire that never shall be quenched: Where their worm dieth not, and the fire is not quenched." Listen to me. If there is no hell, this book is a liar and these holy men of old are all liars. If there is no hell, Jesus was a impostor and the greatest liar of all ages. Jesus spoke about hell. In fact, He talked more about hell than He did about heaven. If there is no hell, Jesus died in vain. The cross was a mistake. Calvary was a failure. But Jesus spoke about hell. It was Jesus who told the story of the rich man and Lazarus. If there is no hell, there is no heaven. The same Bible that tells of the glories and happiness in heaven also describes the doom, the despair, and the anguish of those who die unsaved. The rich man in our text was being tormented by the flames of hell. If there is no hell as some claim, then there is no heaven. The Bible plainly teaches, the moment you die, you go to one of two places. Don't be fooled, my unsaved friend. Today, the Old Serpent is gaping for you right now and hell's mouth is wide open to receive you and if Almighty God should permit it, you would be swallowed up in a moment and lost forever.

The second thing I want to point out to you is that hell is a place of suffering. In Luke 16:24, the rich man cried out, "I am tormented in this flame." So hell is a place of suffering. A person will be consciousness in hell. O how horrible to see, but to see nothing but the flames of hell and men suffering. You will hear, but O how horrible to hear nothing but the groans and shrieks of the lost and doomed forever and ever.

In hell, sinners have complete separation from God and His people. There is coming a time when there will be a separation of the saved from the unsaved. Hearts that are hardened to the message of God will be fixed forever. There will be no hope for a better place. There will be no rest, no water, no light. The Bible says in Matthew 22:13 they will be cast, "into outer darkness." For those that have trampled under their foot the plan of Salvation and rejected God's love there will be no escape. They will be forever sealed in hell. Forever doomed in hell.

Listen to me. A son will point his finger in his father's face and say, "Dad, you led me here. You taught me how to drink and gamble, but you failed to tell me where it would lead me." A daughter will say to her mother, "You taught me how to dress, dance, smoke, and sip cocktails, but you failed to tell me how to die." Yes, there will be weeping and wailing and gnashing of teeth. The flames of hell will burn forever.

The third thing that is going to make hell so horrible is memory. In hell you will remember how some people pleaded with you to accept Jesus Christ. But now it is too late. The rich man had memory. He remembered Lazarus. He remembered in this life he had good eyes which he could have used to read God's word, but now they were tormented by the flames of fire. He remembered his tongue which he could have used to speak for Almighty God, but now was parched by the heat of hell. He remembered his voice which he could have used to sing praises to Almighty God, but now all he could do was scream for mercy.

You will have memory so that across your mind will flash these words from Galatians 6:7, "Whatsoever a man soweth, that shall he also reap." You will perhaps say, "No, I never intended to come here, I had other plans. I really thought my plans would work, but death came when I wasn't expecting it."

The fourth thing I want you to notice is the inhabitance of hell. Who will be in hell? Psalm 9:17 says, "The wicked shall be turned into hell, and all the nations that forget God." If you go to hell, let me tell you who your next door neighbors will be. All atheist will be there. All those who deny God. All those who reject the words of God's blessed book, the Holy Bible. Hitler and his gang that brought death to thousands in Europe during World War II will be there. In John 14:6 the Bible says, "I am the way, the truth, and the life: no man cometh unto the

Father, but by me." All of those who reject Jesus as their personal Saviour will die in their sins. You may be saying, "But I am pretty good. I go to church and give to support missions. That will not save you.

The fifth and last thing I want to say is there is a way to keep out of hell. God made a way for every hell–deserving sinner to be saved. The price was paid over two thousand years ago when Jesus Christ suffered and died on the cross. Six long hours Jesus hung there on the cross with the guilt of our sins upon Him. He died, the just for the unjust, the righteous for the unrighteous, that we might be brought to Almighty God. Almighty God was satisfied with His son's death on the cross.

Religion will not save you. Moral life will not save you. It takes the blood of Jesus to cleanse us from sin. 1 John 1:9 says, "If we confess our sins, he is faithful and just to forgive us our sins, and to cleanse us from all unrighteousness." The old gospel song "Nothing But The Blood" by Robert Lowry says, "What can wash away my sin? Nothing but the blood of Jesus; What can make me whole again? Nothing but the blood of Jesus."

Paul and Silas were cast into prison for preaching the gospel. At midnight there was a great earthquake and the prison doors were shook open and the bands on Paul and Silas fell off. The jailer found that Paul and Silas had not escaped, so he came trembling and fell at Paul's and Silas' feet and said, "Sirs, what must I do to be saved?" (Acts 16:30). They said, "Believe on the Lord Jesus Christ, and thou shalt be saved, and thy house" (Acts 16:31). That is all you have to do.

What will you do today? Will you turn your back upon Him or will you let Him forgive your sins so that you can escape hell. Which will you do? It is left up to you. It is your decision. You have the power to choose and only you can do that. You may not always have the opportunity to make the decision. Revelation 3:20 says, "Behold, I stand at the door, and knock: if any man hear my voice, and open the door, I will come in to him, and will sup with him, and he with me." Surely you don't want to go to hell. Open that door and ask Jesus to forgive your sins and cleanse you right now. What He has done for others, He will do for you. (See Romans 10:9–13).

In the twenty–first chapter of Numbers there is a story of Almighty God sending fiery serpents among the children of Israel while they were wandering in the wilderness because they had rebelled against Him. These serpents were biting the people and the people were falling dead all over their camp. They cried out to Moses for help. The Lord God told Moses to make a serpent of brass and put it on a pole in the middle of the camp and if the people would look up to that serpent of brass on the pole, they would be healed. The Israelites did not have to do anything else but to look at the brass serpent on the pole and they would be healed. All you have to do to be healed of the bite of sin is look to Jesus.

Chapter 33

She's Worth More Than Jewels

As I grew out of my college years, I focused on my potential life ministry and how it could be nurtured with proper planning. Working my way through Georgetown College I admired young women for their talents used for the glory of God in the ministry. In my heart I searched for qualities that could be used in the evangelistic field, perhaps someone who could fill the role of a pastor's wife in Kentucky. With those values in view, I went on to pastor in Eastern Kentucky. Was there one in view?

With God's hand carefully guiding, I met Oleta through my dear friend Rev. W. L. Crumpler. Oleta liked my serious plans for life in God's work and I liked her sense of purpose and commitment to God. I was careful to clearly point out the hardships and unfamiliar lifestyle we would encounter in the upcoming mountain ministry where hollows and creeks prevailed, and starkly independent folk fiercely guarded their homeland. She would have to partner with poverty, souls needing the gospel, and family moves as God commanded. Oleta was prepared, eager, and ready.

Our wedding trip was indeed an extension of the ministry itself, and our life's mission continued without skipping a beat. Oleta was quick to learn and experienced. As a new wife, she directed her focus to the women's and children's programs. With a heart for missions, Oleta quickly introduced to the women the Woman's Missionary Union (WMU), a missions branch of the Southern Baptist Convention. Under Oleta's guidance, the women learned to spot a need and find a way to fill it. Locally they fed and clothed the needy. They learned about missions in foreign countries as well as in our country. They encouraged their families to put aside a little money for the Lottie Moon and Annie Armstrong annual missionary funds.

Oleta worked diligently with Vacation Bible School (VBS), which introduced new families to the church. Being highly organized, she was efficient in using her staff productively, overseeing the curriculum and materials needed, and mastered a plan to get the children into VBS.

Possessing a natural affinity for children, Oleta usually oversaw the Children's Sunday School and Children's Church programs. Her room decorations and crafts caught the attention of many and she freely shared her ideas and materials. She was an excellent teacher, using many visual materials.

She actively participated in the women's classes and projects, and liberally offered her assistance. She had a vision for the future of ministries and trained teachers and WMU leaders.

Oleta had learned early to live on a frugal budget. She rose to the occasion during our early years in Appalachia. She tended a garden, canned a good deal of the harvest, sewed and mended clothing, decorated on a shoe-string budget, stretched many a meal to include others, and kept our financial books.

Chapter 33 — She's Worth More Than Jewels

Oleta was always there when I needed her, but she knew that the ministry was top priority. She was careful not to disturb the time, spaces, and attention I needed to carry out God's work. She filled in wherever she could. She took courses to learn about office management, office machines, school issues, and any other classes she could find to help me out and fill various vacancies as they occurred.

After we retired, we became Florida State Volunteers for the American Bible Society in Florida. Together we distributed thousands of Bibles and tracts ministering to churches, truckers, migrants and numerous organizations. Oleta often worked at fairs, conferences, and public meetings where she setup a booth and evangelized for the American Bible Society, WMU, and activities sponsored by the Southern Baptists.

A friend of mine once asked me what made Oleta and me so happy and successful. I simply replied that God was our tour guide and we are along for the ride. Nether Oleta nor I have tried to wave our own flag; we were simply doing what our God has called us to do.

There were many times in our lives when we really did struggle. Our income was very low and we did without luxuries and things many folks consider necessities. During these times we would turn to the book of Acts and read how the apostles, who had previously sought their own glory, now sought only to serve Almighty God. After reading these words, we could not complain. We decided to follow God by faith and by faith alone. Pleasing God meant that we trust Him not only to direct our church work but our entire family life. We believed that Almighty God delighted in rewarding His faithful servants. (See Ephesians 6:7–8, Galatians 6:9, Matthew 7:7–8, and Corinthians 2:9).

We may face problems, difficulties, hardships, and humiliation along life's way but if we have the risen Christ in us, success will never be about what we can acquire in life. Instead, it becomes about what we can give away. To pursue God's best, we must abandon the earthly rewards and press on as did the Apostle Paul. (See 2 Timothy 4:6–8).

Oleta and I read in the Bible where Joshua's success depended upon his obedience to God's Word. The same is true for us today. (See Joshua 1:1–9).

I remember the first time I saw Oleta Lancaster, it was in the basement of the Central Baptist Church at Maysville, Kentucky. She was sitting in the basement of the church folding bulletins.

The tie that bound Oleta's life and mine so closely together was a tie in the Lord Jesus. It was by far stronger than any earthly tie and when she died, her going would have been unbearable had it not been for our Lord and His inspired and Holy Word.

To have a home on this earth is a wonderful thing. It is a place to go when you are tired. It is a place of contentment and comfort. However, our Heavenly home is one of the best places our human mind can comprehend. We Christians will be with

Chapter 33 — She's Worth More Than Jewels

our Saviour, the Lord Jesus Christ, forever. Oleta has now seen Moses, Abraham, Peter, and all the other redeemed of all ages.

I want to put into words what contributed to Oleta's success as a born again believer in Jesus Christ. First, Oleta never lost sight of the fact that she was a sinner saved by grace. She did not doubt that she had a genuine experience of grace. No matter where we travelled people were convinced that she was soundly saved.

Next, she never lost sight of the fact that she had a call from Almighty god to share her faith in her Saviour. People who got to know her were convinced she was one of God's great disciples.

Thirdly, Oleta never lost sight of the fact that all people, every where, were lost and needed a Saviour.

Fourth, she loved the church and was devoted to it until the very end.

Finally, she believed Jesus was preparing a home for her in heaven. His home was more real to her than her earthly home. There is no greater joy than the peace and assurance of knowing that, whatever the future may hold, you are secure in the loving arms of Jesus Christ.

Jesus Christ is our hope right now. He is our hope for the future. Even in the midst of all the storms that may come our way, Jesus Christ can give us a inner peace and joy.

In summary, Oleta doesn't live here any more. She moved out of her earthly house and into the City of God. She is now in the presence of God, and she is in company with the angels and the redeemed of all ages. She is alive and inexpressibly happy.

Oleta was not perfect in this life, but I do believe she served her Lord and Saviour with all her heart for the Lord's glory.

Oleta Frances Lancaster Casey died, after several bouts with cancer, on November 14, 2011. She was buried at the Maysville–Mason County Cemetery located in her hometown of Maysville, Kentucky. News of her death recalled memories by many. The following excerpts are tributes in her remembrance.

"...His preparation for us in heaven over the past 2000 years will be beyond what we could ever imagine. This is our glorious hope."

Dr. David Jeremiah
Turning Point
San Diego, California
February 15, 2012

In her memory, generous gifts were given to Main Street Baptist Church in Williamsburg, Kentucky, to "keep the memory of Oleta for years to come." Donations were also given to Hospice of the Bluegrass–Mountain Heritage in Pikeville, Kentucky, so they might continue their benevolent work. In honor of Oleta's love for missions, a generous gift was given to the Lottie Moon Ministry of 2011. "Oleta would be pleased to know that missions giving continues in her name." A donation was given to the Kentucky Baptist Children's Home in memory of Oleta's love for children. In addition, numerous Bibles were donated through the Gideons in Kentucky.

A special "Thank you" is in order to Henry F. Haas of Mount Dora, Florida. A long-time friend of ours, Henry stood on-hand as a great organizer in times of need for prayer. He was very encouraging when Oleta and I were struggling with health problems, providing prayer, needs, and gifts.

The Boy From Back CreekJames E. Casey, Jr.

The Light Of My Life

I will always remember her first sight.
She was a beautiful and winsome delight.
Her joy and radiant smile were breathtaking,
While her Christian character was overwhelming.

She soon knew how to win my love and heart.
Her thoughts were true and pure from the start.
She was always gentle, calm and care free.
Her love for God's work was constant and easy to see.

My life has been blessed from the beginning to the end.
Thank you Lord for the beautiful light you did send.
The sweet joy and love has been really wonderful.
May this light continue to shine as we walk toward Heaven.

Happy Birthday
Beautiful Light
Oleta

Love, Jim
September 4, 2004

Epilogue

It has not been the purpose of this book to identify all the different programs and patterns with kaleidoscopic speed that the Boy from Back Creek and the Girl from 531 Pelham Street used but rather to show how faith in Almighty God led us to spread the gospel no matter where we were located.

Over and over we hear people ask questions like these : "Why can't I have success in my work?" "Is there something causing my failures?" It is the assumption of many people in our society that success is found in monetary gain. There are others who say the cause of world tension is wrapped up in the lack of knowledge. Finally, it is the assumption of others that the environment, such as poor living conditions, is the breeding ground of evil and trouble.

Whatever the circumstances in the world or in our lives, we can be successful in spreading the Word of God. Whatever our talents, monetary positions, cultures, God's plan for us can develop us to our full potential. He will open ways for us to harvest for His Kingdom.

Whatever gifts He gives us, they are enough to accomplish His goals for us. My God wants to meet your needs as you travel through life. (See Psalm 37:3–4). If God has called you to do something, He will supply all your needs. You will be given the strength and basic needs to do God's work He has called you to do. (See Philippians 4:12). If we abide in Him, He will fill us with power to be successful. We will be encouraged and encourage others. He will enhance our eyes and hearts and minds to understand our assignments from God and act on them diligently.

And pray! Almighty God takes you seriously when you pray. Pray for God's leading, pray for His work, pray for souls, pray that your testimony be true, and pray God's will be done.

Christians must never fall into the traps that come along life's pathways. Many people in the Western Culture are too preoccupied with material things and miss out on many of Almighty God's big blessings. Almighty God wants His children to just trust Him and Him alone as we travel through this troubled world. The God of the Old Testament is the God of today. If God could make a path through the Red Sea for Moses and the Israelites to walk on, He can take care of His children today. John 14:1 says, "Let not your heart be troubled." Leave everything in God's hands and enjoy the trip while on planet earth.

May G. Onishchuk

Appendix

Co-Laborers Give Their Perspectives

Correspondence One

This is a brief history of Dr. James E. Casey, Jr.

Dr. Casey was born on September 4, 1930, and Dr. Lester Collins of Mount Eden, Kentucky, was the physician. He spent his childhood days on the Back Creek Road. He walked to school the first three years to a old school in Mount Eden, Kentucky. In 1939 a new school was built and bus transportation was then provided.

In a old fashioned revival meeting in October of 1942, Jim Casey was converted and baptized into the Mount Moriah Baptist Church in Mount Eden, Kentucky. Jim graduated as a valedictorian of the 1948 class of Mount Eden High School. Jim Casey surrendered to preach on June 10, 1951, and was licensed to preach on June 10, 1951, by the Mount Moriah Baptist Church, Mount Eden, Kentucky, Grant Jones, Pastor. He entered Georgetown College, Georgetown, Kentucky, in September of 1951 and graduated with the B. A. degree in August 13, 1954.

He married Oleta Lancaster of Maysville, Kentucky, and they had four children.

The Rev. Mr. Casey holds degrees from Luther Rice Seminary and the International Bible Institute. He conducted two soul saving revival meetings at the Mount Moriah Baptist Church during his long years of evangelistic ministry. Dr. Casey served churches in Kentucky, Indiana, and Florida as Pastor. For 12 1/2 years he was Director of Missions in the Russell Creek and East Lynn Baptist Associations and lived in Greensburg, Kentucky.

In 1992 he and his wife retired to Florida where he worked with the American Bible Society as Florida State Coordinator until March 14, 2007. James and Oleta were dedicated servants of the Lord Jesus Christ.

Donald Husband
Mount Moriah Baptist Church
Mount Eden, Kentucky

Correspondence Two

Dear Brother Casey,

Sorry I haven't written before now. Trying to gather up some information for you. I guess I still have a little more time for you book. I do understand as you said it may be used and may not.

I met you I in 1954 in McRoberts, Kentucky. We have always kept in touch of course. When my sister's three month old baby passed away it was a sad time. A sad time. The funeral service was at Ester and Dulcina Gibson's and you being a young pastor. We continued to keep in touch and I followed your ministry all through the years. I grew to know Oleta more and more through the years. You and Oleta helped me so much with my Christian walk with my Lord Jesus. How precious our Lord God Almighty is. You and your wife sent me so many letters and pamphlets and poems. I was so sorry to hear about Oleta's passing away in November. We know it gives us peace to know our loved ones are in Heaven and a day at a time God will ease our hurt and sorrow and pain. He is our rock and shield. In him we put our trust and faith. I praise God for you and Oleta. This is some article about you and Oleta.

Love in Jesus your sister,
Wilma Gibson–Hare
Fayetteville, North Carolina

Correspondence Three

More than 20 years ago, two men met who would become lifelong friends. Bro. Casey and Virgil had lots in common including age and birth month. Bro. Casey was then Director of Missions for East Lynn as well as Russell Creek Baptist Associations. Through his ministry, Virgil got to know him well and they spent time together on the road witnessing for the Lord.

Bro. Casey was the inspiration for Virgil's first mission trip abroad which led to many more. Bro. Casey and his wife have been blessings to many lives. Mrs. Casey may have been a quiet, behind the scenes type but served through WMU for several years.

Some locals paid tribute to the Casey's by traveling to Leesburg, Florida on mission to provide construction work on the church Bro. Casey was pastoring at the time.

Famous Bro. Casey quotes we still remember:

"I've never had a blue Monday."

"Keep the main thing the main thing."

Virgil and Frances Noe
(Mike and Patty Nunn,
and Troy and Lorie Hawkins)
Greensburg, Kentucky

Correspondence Four

I thank our Lord for the faithful and dedicated ministry of Brother James Casey when he served as Pastor of Beattyville Baptist Church and his missionary ministry throughout Lee County, Kentucky. When I was Pastor of Heidelberg Baptist Church, Brother Casey and the Beattyville congregation wanted to help us. Since we didn't have office equipment, they offered the use of theirs. I would go to their church office and make copies of our Sunday bulletins and other materials. That was a special blessing to us at Heidelberg. I still appreciate Brother Casey very much for his interest and concern. He continues to encourage and uplift my spirit. I thank our Lord for his Biblical knowledge and for the devotions and studies he sends me even now in my life.

James F. Smith
Pastor 1963–1976
Heidelberg Baptist Church, Kentucky

Correspondence Five

When I was growing up, my cousin Jim Casey (or June as we called him) was fifteen years older than I so we didn't have much in common. I do remember as he began his ministry, he would always come to visit us once or twice a year. He would sleep over on the sofa, take us for a ride in his "neat" car and my mom would always prepare a special meal.

After he married and started raising his family I remember hearing how Oleta was such a hard worker. I remember my mother telling us after attending church on Sunday, she gave birth on Mon. or Tues. and was back in church on the following Sunday with the newborn.

As the years went by and Jim and Oleta moved to Florida, we didn't see them much. I remember the day Uncle Elmo sold his house in Mt. Eden. Following the sale Jim and Oleta took Aunt Edna and Uncle Elmo back to Florida to live near them.

In 2002 my brother and sisters and I planned a trip to visit Uncle Elmo at his home in Florida. Once there he showed us around his retirement home. Then we headed off to visit Jim and Oleta a short distance away in Grand Island.

When we arrived we were treated like royalty. Lyndon and his family, and Barry and his family were also there. Oleta had prepared us this special meal of lasagna, salad and bread, and homemade dessert. I will never forget how sweet and kind she was to us and we just had such a special time. They showed us around their home and we went outside and Jim gave us oranges from his tree. We took many photos that day which I will always cherish.

I will never forget that visit and also when they moved to Williamsburg. Oleta always welcomed us into their home and treated everyone so kind. She had a wonderful heart.

I am very proud of Jim and his ministry and all that God has blessed him with.

I look forward to reading his book.

Judy Turner
Shelbyville, Kentucky

Correspondence Six

We were blessed to have Rev. James Casey as pastor of the Swiss Colony Baptist Church. His wife, Oleta, with her gentle nature and sweet smile, and their four children were bonus Caseys. When Pastor Casey was here he was the talk of our rural community. He was up early and still going strong after long hours each day. He was often out visiting, finding and inviting to church people we did not realize were in the community or had given up on getting into church. We always said, "That Brother Casey can find 'em under the rocks." If all the couples served the Lord with the faithfulness of the Casey's, we would be happy to watch the evening news for ours would be a different world.

Hank and Alma Wilson
Previous Pastor
Swiss Colony Baptist Church, Kentucky

Correspondence Seven

Jim Casey is a friend in the ministry for many years. Our days in Florida, then our joint efforts in the ministry in Kentucky and Ohio have offered great opportunities for me to witness his effectiveness, his total commitment to spreading the Good News to all people.

Joe and Carolyn Crumpler
Cincinnati, Ohio

Correspondence Eight

Dear Jim,

Thank you for your volunteer ministry with the American Bible Society. My memories of you are closely bound with my memories of you and Oleta as a team, working together side–by–side in perfect harmony—and always with a smile! I remember you as someone we could always count on to have made all of the necessary preparations for the ABS conferences in your area. Under your watch care, everything always moved along smoothly. Jean joins me in thanking you—and Oleta in memoriam—for you firm friendship throughout the years, as well as your absolute dedication to the cause of Christ, especially through your volunteer ministry with the American Bible Society.

Barclay M. Newman
American Bible Society, Missouri

Correspondence Nine

Jim and Oleta Casey have exemplified dedication to the Lord through their many years in Christian ministry together. The Caseys served in Florida, and we in Ohio, as Volunteer State Partnership Coordinators. Their concern was to make the Gospel known to everyone who could possibly be reached. We witnessed their tireless efforts to this end.

Evelyn and Orville Nichols
American Bible Society, Ohio

Correspondence Ten

My wife, Lucille, and I feel very blessed to count Rev. and Mrs. Casey as dear friends. He served as Associational Missionary for Russell Creek and East Lynn Association in Kentucky for several years. Dr. Casey was one of the hardest workers, always busy, and encouraging others to labor in the

Lord's work. He and Oleta were an inspiration to everyone they met.

Rev. Irvin and Lucille Milby
Summersville, Kentucky

Correspondence Eleven

Dear Jim and Oleta,

What a pleasure it has been to serve with you both at Grand Island Baptist Church. You both have been so constant in your service to the Lord. I appreciate your constant support and encouragement. As a young pastor, it is good t hear your words of affirmation. Oleta, I must tell you how much I appreciate your work in Missions and with the children. JulieAnn has told me over and over how much she has appreciated your work with her. You two are special people and you will be specially missed around Grand Island Baptist Church.

Don and JulieAnn Feezor
Pastor
Grand Island Baptist Church, Florida

Correspondence Twelve

I have some pleasant childhood memories of my mom and dad, Cordia and Everett Casey, my sisters Jane and Judy, brother Bobby, (my brother Don was not born until I was in high school) and I visiting Uncle Elmo Casey and his family on their farm. We enjoyed spending an occasional Sunday afternoon there with Uncle Elmo, Aunt Edna, and Cousin Louise and Cousin Jim, who we always called "June." It was especially fun to ride Uncle Elmo's ponies.

Later on, visits to Uncle Elmo's farm were fun when Jim and Oleta would be there and Louise and her husband Charles. As time went on their children added to the fun.

One summer in the late sixties or early seventies Jim was spending a few days with Uncle Elmo and Aunt Edna. At that time my husband Ernie and I and our sons Steve and Russ were living in Waddy and attending Waddy Baptist Church. Jim was scheduled to speak at Cedarmore Baptist Assembly one evening. This is the Kentucky Baptist Convention state camp and he was to share about one of his mission trips. We were having bible school at our church and I arranged with Jim and the VBS director for Jim to come and share with our VBS children about his experiences on that mission trip. What a blessing it was for our VBS children to meet and hear directly from a "real live" missionary.

In the Fall of 1989, Ernie and I made our first of three mission trips to Espírito Santo, Brazil. We were part of the first team of eight to go with the Kentucky/Brazil Partnership which was a five year partnership.

At that time Jim and Oleta were living in Greensburg in Green County, Kentucky. Jim was serving as Associational Directory of Missions. Jim invited us down twice to share about our experience and promote the partnership at associational meetings. My mother Cordia Casey went down with use once and we visited Jim in his and Oleta's home until time to go to the dinner and meeting. Oleta was in Florida with their son Lyndon, who was recovering from a serious back injury.

I'll always remember what a warm welcome we received from the folks in Greensburg. It was obvious we they had a lot of love and respect for Jim and Oleta. Later in the partnership Jim went with a team to the same area in Brazil that we served in.

Joyce Cloyd
Bagdad, Kentucky

Correspondence Thirteen

[On May 18, 1955, at the age of twenty–four, I was pastor of the McRoberts Baptist Church, McRoberts, Kentucky, and gave a Bible to this boy who was graduating from high school. Forty–three years later I spoke on the phone with this boy, who is now a man. Below is the letter he wrote me.]

18 May '98

Dear Rev. Casey:

Enjoyed my conversation with you this morning. I have often wondered what happened with your life after I last had contact with you on 18 May 1955.

I have the Bible you gave to me on that day and I am forever grateful for your kindness. The "Good News" has traveled with me the last forty-three years.

As I said, you gave us a sense of pride and purpose back in 1955. You always treated young people in a fair and just manner. You were a fine young minister and a somewhat good basketball coach—at least we seem to win games! You were an excellent role model to teenagers growing up in a small coal mining town in the '50s.

Best to you.

Ronald L. Crosbie
Huntington, West Virginia

Correspondence Fourteen

I first met Rev. Jim Casey when he served as interim pastor at Sorrento Baptist Church. I had never seen a more dedicated and hard-working pastor. He was then seventy-five years old, yet traveling almost daily to visit our congregation. We shared many visits with him and Oleta both in Kentucky and Florida. We met his father who was one hundred years old at the time and we also had the honor to visit Oleta when she was bedfast. Jim and Oleta are two of the most precious people we have had the pleasure of knowing.

Larry and Dessie Calhoun
Apopka, Florida

Correspondence Fifteen

Thank you for offering your services to the New Work Team of the Lake County Baptist Association for a decade during your retirement years. You also assisted in preaching and interim work with several churches. Many speak fondly of Oleta's help in WMU, our county fair ministry, and our mobile dental clinic. It is becoming more difficult to find leaders who have a heart for missions and who work together cooperatively. As I spoke with you, I appreciated I was sharing with someone who was first a Christian and second a Southern Baptist. I count it an honor to have known and served with you and Oleta in the ongoing Kingdom Ministry.

Donald Miller
Lake County Baptist Association, Florida

Correspondence Sixteen

Dr. James E. Casey and his late beloved wife Oleta have been used by our Lord to make His Word known to many in our country and abroad. The Caseys, as we've referred to them throughout the years, blessed everyone they come in contact with. The selfless giving of their talent, time and treasure as volunteers for American Bible Society have guided many people to come to faith in Christ. Their ministry is a testimony of Christ followers who, not only engage with the Bible, but extend it to others. sister Oleta is already in heaven enjoying the fruit of her labor. It is up to us to emulate the Casey's testimony by putting God's Word into action.

Rev. Emilio A. Reyes
Vice President, Multi–Language Ministries
American Bible Society, Florida

Correspondence Seventeen

Bro. James E. Casey, Jr. was hired as the Director of Missions for the Russell Creek Association of Kentucky Baptist in March of 1980 and began his duties in that position in July of 1980. The Casey's purchased a home on East Locust Street in Greensburg and lived there for the duration of his time here. Bro. Casey remodeled the basement garage of his home and used it as the Association office. Prior to that time the Director of Missions did not have an office as such. They worked out of their home and rotated among some churches that provided a small room to use as a make shift office. Bro. Casey was given permission by the Executive Board of the Russell Creek Association in January of 1982 to work on a part time basis with the East Lynn Association, and actually began his duties there in July of 1982. He continued his role as Director of Missions bro both the Russell Creek and East Lynn Associations until the time of his official retirement on December 31, 1992.

Bro. Casey and his family were members of the Greensburg Baptist Church in Greensburg, Kentucky. Bro. Casey attended when he could, but many of his Sundays he was visiting, preaching, or ministering in various churches in both Associations. Mrs. Oleta Casey was an active member of the church. She was very involved in Sunday School, Woman's Missionary Union, and Bible Schools. She also served as Associational WMU Director in 1986–87. She served as a part–time hourly secretary for the Association beginning in 1988. (I assume she did this work until their retirement because I could find no other person hired for the job.) Mrs. Casey was employed as a part time Women, Infants, and Children Supplemental Food Program clerk for the Lake Cumberland District Health Department, Green County Health Center, from August 1982 until September 1993. She worked wonderfully with the economically deprived young mothers. (I personally was a co–worker with her for this entire period).

Some of the highlights/significant events of Bro. Casey's time of Director of Missions include the following:

Began publishing the Russell Creek Association newsletter in the Western Recorder in 1985.

Bro. Casey organized a World Missions Conference held in the fall of 1986.

Helped organize and promote simultaneous revivals with twenty churches participating in the spring of 1986.

Bro. and Mrs. Casey took a mission trip to Kenya in 1987. The East Lynn Association contributed one thousand dollars to help construct churches there; and the Youth of the Russell

Creek raised five thousand three hundred dollars to help construct churches.

In 1985 a mission endeavor to the Enterprise Association in Eastern Kentucky was undertaken.

Bro. Casey helped organize and formed a long term relationship with the Steel Valley Association of Ohio Baptist in 1986. Five men from the Russell Creek Association traveled there and worked with them.

A World Mission Conference was held in 1989.

Bro. Casey and another pastor (Bro. Gary Ervin) took the initiative to get a history of both the Russell Creek and East Lynn Associations published in 1989.

Bro. Casey took a mission trip to Brazil in 1991.

Bro. Casey organized a World Mission Conference to be held in 1993.

Bro. James Casey and Mrs. Oleta Casey were faithful, dedicated servants of the Lord. Bro. Casey worked diligently to promote missions—local, state, and worldwide. His work fostered a spirit of harmony and cooperation among the churches he served.

Clifford Cook
Clerk, Russell Creek Baptist Association
Greensburg, Kentucky

www.ingramcontent.com/pod-product-compliance
Lightning Source LLC
Chambersburg PA
CBHW032100090426
42743CB00007B/190